Conflicts in the Middle East since 1945

Since the Second World War, conflicts such as the Iran–Iraq War and the second Gulf War have made the Middle East the main focus of military attention. *Conflicts in the Middle East* analyses the nature of conflict in the Middle East, with its racial, ethnic, political, cultural, religious and economic factors.

Giving a much-needed historical overview, the main conflicts are also put in their wider context with a thematic debate of issues such as:

- The emergence of radical Islam
- The resolution of conflicts
- Diplomacy and peacemaking
- The role of the superpowers

Revised throughout, the second edition of this successful book brings the history of conflict in the Middle East up to date. Including a brand new chapter, this edition examines the effects of 9/11 and the second Gulf War on the Middle East peace process. The authors also consider how these events may affect conflict in the Middle East in the future.

Conflicts in the Middle East is an indispensable introduction to modern Middle Eastern history for undergraduates and the general reader alike.

Beverley Milton-Edwards is Reader in the School of Politics and Assistant Director for Study of Ethnic Conflict at Queen's University Belfast. She is the author of *Islamic Politics in Palestine* (1996) and *Contemporary Politics in the Middle East* (1999).

Peter Hinchcliffe is an Honorary Senior Research Fellow in the School of Politics at Queen's University Belfast and an Honorary Research Fellow at the University of Edinburgh. He is co-author of *Jordan: a Hashemite Legacy* (2000) with Beverley Milton-Edwards and a former British Ambassador to Kuwait and Jordan.

The Making of the Contemporary World
Edited by Eric J. Evans and Ruth Henig

The Making of the Contemporary World series provides challenging interpretations of contemporary issues and debates within strongly defined historical frameworks. The range of the series is global, with each volume drawing together material from a range of disciplines – including economics, politics and sociology. The books in this series present compact, indispensable introductions for students studying the modern world.

Conflicts in the Middle East since 1945

Second Edition

**Beverley Milton-Edwards
and Peter Hinchcliffe**

 Routledge
Taylor & Francis Group

LONDON AND NEW YORK

First published 2001
Reprinted 2002 (twice)

Second edition first published 2004
by Routledge
11 New Fetter Lane, London EC4P 4EE

Simultaneously published in the USA and Canada
by Routledge
29 West 35th Street, New York, NY 10001

Routledge is an imprint of the Taylor & Francis Group

© 2001, 2004 Beverley Milton-Edwards and Peter Hinchcliffe

Typeset in Times by Keystroke, Jacaranda Lodge, Wolverhampton
Printed and bound in Great Britain by TJ International Ltd, Padstow, Cornwall

British Library Cataloguing in Publication Data
A catalogue record for this book is available from the British Library

Library of Congress Cataloging in Publication Data
Milton-Edwards, Beverley.
  Conflicts in the Middle East since 1945 / Beverley Milton-Edwards and
Peter Hinchcliffe.—2nd ed.
      p.   cm.—(Making of the contemporary world)
Includes bibliographical references and index.
1. Middle East—Politics and government—1945– 2. Mediation,
International. I. Hinchcliffe, Peter, 1937– II. Title. III. Series.
  DS63.1.M566 2003
  956.04—dc21

                                                           2003012408

ISBN 0–415–31786–X (hbk)
ISBN 0–415–31787–8 (pbk)

To the children of conflict

Contents

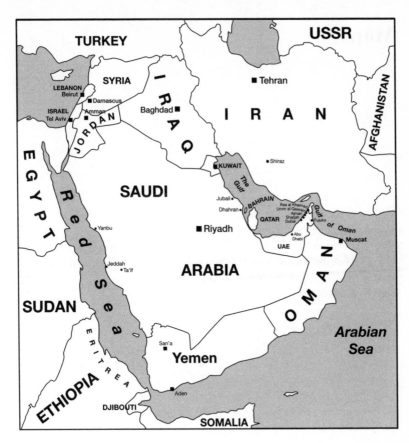

Map A – Middle East and Gulf

Maps

Preface

The first edition of this book was written before a series of momentous events that have coloured the first years of the twenty-first century. They have placed new pressures on the forces for peace and conflict in the Middle East region and the impact that the politics of this region has on the wider international order. We have accordingly modified this book to take account of such events as the '9/11' al-Qaeda attacks on America, the subsequent American declaration of global war on terrorism, the invasion of Iraq, and the virtual collapse of the Middle East peace process within the Oslo framework. By revising this work for a new edition we are also able to take account of the useful criticism of earlier readers and users of this text. For example, we have expanded Chapter 3 on superpower rivalry and refined the following one on conflict in the name of Islam. Minor revisions on the chapters dealing with the Kurds, following the overthrow of Saddam's regime in Iraq, and with the progress of peace after civil war and Israeli withdrawal in Lebanon reflect changing circumstances.

We are generous with our definition of the Middle East and the territories and peoples who have been affected by conflicts since 1945. In the interest of brevity we have concentrated on the more important events so some war zones such as the Sudan, Eritrea and the Western Sahara, for instance, are not featured. In this respect we are not entirely bound to territories or state but seek to explain conflict in terms of other actors such as social or religious ones. We concentrate on territories, however, that have been badly scarred by conflicts of a very modern variety. All too often conflicts are about modern boundaries and barriers, but we choose to overcome them in presenting a different style of analysis in this book.

This text is aimed at a variety of readers. We aspire to open up what appear to be complex and intractable conflicts to readers who are motivated by a variety of reasons to know more about the region and its political dynamics. Our original concept was to produce a book for an undergraduate audience, but perhaps because of renewed interest in Middle Eastern affairs and in

Islam, triggered off by 9/11, the book has proved popular with the general reader, becoming something of a best seller.

So much has been written about dispute and conflict, war and peace-making in the Middle East. The Arab–Israeli conflict, the dimensions of the Palestinian–Israeli battle, the two Gulf wars (Iraq/Iran and the Kuwait war), Lebanon, the Kurds, the 'rise' of political Islam have all demanded explanation, historical record and, often, competing perspectives in terms of explaining why collapse into violence has occurred in such contexts. The need for an accessible synthesis tying together all the complex and tangled skeins has been apparent for some time. It is our aspiration that this book goes some way in meeting such a need.

Acknowledgements

The co-authors of this book would like to thank David Evans and Ruth Henig for their encouragement during this project. We hope it will offer some critical insight into a variety of conflicts associated with the region which might be unfamiliar to the first time reader. This project in itself has encouraged us to remain eternal students of the region, making new discoveries and new friendships along the way. We would like to extend our gratitude to Gillian Oliver and Alex Ballantine at Routledge who have encouraged us to embark on this second edition. Our thanks also to the many friends within the region and those we made during the writing of this book, including British Foreign and Commonwealth Office Staff in Jordan, Tel Aviv and East Jerusalem, the Irish 87th Battalion UNIFIL force in South Lebanon, and in particular Chris Moore, Declan Carberry, Joe McDonagh, and Mick Kelly for the expert advice and assistance. The European Union Commission and Council departments for the Middle East and the Office of the Special Envoy to the Middle East Peace Process, including H. E. Miguel Moratinos, have greatly assisted us in this project also. Our thanks are also extended to our colleagues in both the School of Politics at Queen's University of Belfast and the Institute for Arabic and Islamic Studies Edinburgh University, and to those of our students who have played a role in the dialogue about conflict in the Middle East. Our final thanks to our life-long partners Graham and Archie, and to our children who have happily supported us in our endeavours.

Beverley Milton-Edwards
Peter Hinchcliffe
Belfast, May 2003

Chronology

1945 End of Second World War.

1946 Lebanon achieves full independence from France.

1947 (November) UN adopts Partition Plan for Palestine.

1948 (May) The outbreak of the first Arab–Israeli war and birth of the Palestinian refugee issue.

1950 Jordan annexes the West Bank.

1951 (July) King Abdullah of Jordan assassinated at the Temple Mount in Jerusalem.

1952 Free Officer Coup in Egypt. Gamal Abdel Nasser becomes President in 1954.

1956 (October) Suez crisis following nationalization, brings Britain, France and Israel into military confrontation with Egypt.

1957 (January) Eisenhower Doctrine issued by US government.

1958 US marines land in Beirut at request of President Chamoun following widespread disorder.

1963 (March) Ba'ath Party to power in Syria following *coup d'etat*.

1964 The Palestine Liberation Organization founded by Egypt.

1967 (June) Six Day War. Arab armies defeated, Israel occupies Palestinian, Syrian and Egyptian territory.

1968 (January) Fatah, the Palestinian resistance movement led by Yasser Arafat formed.

      (July) Ba'ath Party coup in Iraq.

1970 (September) President Nasser dies and Anwar Sadat becomes president.

      (September) Civil war in Jordan as Palestinian resistance forces and Jordanian armed forces clash.

      (November) Hafez al-Assad becomes President of Syria.

1973 (October) Yom Kippur war brings Egyptian and Syrian troops into confrontation with Israel. Israel defeats the Arab armies once more.

1974 (March) Autonomy foisted on Iraqi Kurds by Saddam Hussein.

1975 (April) Outbreak of the Lebanese civil war.

1976 (January) Syrian army enters Lebanese arena.

1977 (November) President Sadat of Egypt pays historic visit to Jerusalem.

1978 (March) Israeli forces invade Lebanon.

(September) Israel and Egypt sign Camp David Peace Accords. UN establishes multi-national peacekeeping force (UNIFIL) for South Lebanon.

1979 (January) Revolution in Iran. Shah is toppled and Ayatollah Khomeini returns from exile.

1980 (September) Outbreak of the Iran–Iraq War.

1981 (October) President Sadat of Egypt assassinated by Islamic militants.

1982 (June) Israel invades Lebanon.

(September) Massacres in Palestinian refugee camps of Sabra and Shatilla in Lebanon by Phalangist allies of Israel.

1983 (May) Israeli–Lebanese Accords signed.

1984 (March) Israeli–Lebanese Accords abrogated.

1985 (January) Israel withdraws some troops from Lebanon.

1986 (April) US raid on Libyan capital of Tripoli.

1987 (December) The outbreak of the Palestinian uprising (Intifada).

1988 (March) Iraq uses chemical weapons on Iraqi Kurds at Halabja.

(July) King Hussein abrogates annexation of West Bank.

(August) Ceasefire agreed between Iran and Iraq.

1989 (October) Ta'if Peace Agreement brings civil war in Lebanon to an end.

1990 (August) Saddam Hussein orders Iraqi troops to invade and occupy Kuwait.

1991 (February) Allied Forces successfully end Iraq's occupation of Kuwait. Outbreak of Kurdish and Shi'a Uprisings in Iraq.

(October) First multi-lateral peace conference on the Arab–Israeli dispute held in Madrid.

1993 (September) Israel and the PLO sign the Oslo Accords establishing Palestinian autonomy and agenda for final status negotiations.

1994 (August) Yasser Arafat returns to Gaza.

(October) Israel and Jordan sign a peace treaty ending conflict.

1995 (November) Prime Minister Yitzhak Rabin assassinated by Jewish right-wing fanatic at a Peace rally in Tel Aviv.

1996 (March) Palestinian Islamists embark on a suicide bomb campaign against Israel.

(June) Israelis elect right-wing Likud leader Binjamin 'Bibi' Netanyahu as Prime Minister.

1999 (February) King Hussein of Jordan dies. His son Abdullah is crowned.

(June) Former Army general Ehud Barak elected in Israel as Prime Minister on pro-peace process platform.

2000 (May) Israeli troops withdraw from South Lebanon and its local proxy the South Lebanon Army collapses.

(June) Hafez al-Assad of Syria dies. His son Bashar elected Presidential successor.

(September) Following the visit by Israeli Likud leader to Temple Mount and al-Aqsa mosque in Jerusalem Palestinian protest and Israeli violence leads to a subsequent Israeli declaration of 'time out' from the peace process and the second Intifada is announced.

(October) Al-Qaeda attack on USS *Cole* moored in Yemeni waters.

2001 (September) al-Qaeda, led by Usama Bin Laden, launch attacks on New York and Washington.

(October) Allied alliance begins military operations against Afghanistan.

(November) Kabul falls.

(December) New interim administration led by Hamid Karzai takes power.

2002 (April) Israel reoccupies West Bank and the government of Ariel Sharon declares Yasser Arafat an 'enemy of the state'.

(June) President George W. Bush recognizes that two states must form solution to Palestinian–Israeli conflict.

(November) UNSCR 1441 passed against Iraq and weapons of mass destruction.

2003 (March) War against Iraq launched by Allied forces led by the United States of America.

(April) Baghdad falls and the regime of Saddam Hussein collapses.

'Road map' for Middle East Peace published by the Quartet (the US, UN, EU and Russia) and handed over to the Palestinians and the Israelis.

Introduction

One fundamental question should be asked of many contemporary accounts of the history and politics of the Middle East in the latter half of the twentieth century. Why does so much analysis of the region take as read that the Middle East, unlike most other regions of the globe, is characterized by a Hobbesian state of nature where war and conflicts are inevitable and endemic? This book sets out to address this perception through examining a series of examples by way of a variety of factors and conditions which have given rise to war and conflicts.

Rather than comparing the region with others with a similar history of conflict such as Africa or Latin America, we have kept our focus on the Middle East. Suffice it to say that conflict ridden though this area has been since the Second World War, its history of confrontation and instability is arguably little different than war-torn western and central Africa or the former Yugoslavia. Its also worth recalling that much of the genesis of conflicts in the region has arisen from the same factors such as the legacy of colonialism and superpower rivalry, as in other parts of the globe. Nevertheless, the dominant perception in the West fed by prejudicial images of bloodthirsty Arabs pitted against their enemies or fighting amongst themselves demands an explanation. We have sought to find one in this book without, from the outset, accepting Hobbesian assumptions but seeking instead to find a less 'Orientalist' and more rational explanation for the presence of conflicts within the region.[1]

The Arab–Israeli dispute has been the most dominant and enduring feature of the post-war Middle East. But it is only one of a number of conflicts that this book will address. Conflict in the region is and has been multi-faceted. As we shall explain, it is not just about state-to-state war, the traditional combat between sovereign nation-states in dispute, but also other kinds of tensions. These have led to internal, inter-state and regional conflagration sometimes lasting many decades. Although such conflicts are said to characterize the region and be indicative of its war-mongering peoples, they have, in many cases, roots in the history of persistent inter-vention by outside powers pursuing strategic interests, including access to the area's economic riches – particularly oil.

Indeed we would contend that since 1945 the peoples of the region have often been subjected to some of the most aggressive and predatory policies of outside powers. This is partly, but only partly, explained by superpower rivalry and compounded in the case of the United States by domestic pressures, which have seemingly prevented it exercising its power and influence in an even-handed manner in accordance with gener-ally accepted international norms when dealing with much of the conflict bedevilling the region. On first reading, such an assertion may appear unduly hard, but in the following chapters we will present evidence to support our contention.

We will show how conflict in the Middle East is made manifest in many ways, including actual warfare, political violence, low-intensity conflict, perceived failure of diplomacy, virulent propaganda, political and economic boycotts, disputes over land and water, resistance to occupation and deeply ingrained cultures of antagonism. By the same token we believe the majority of these conflicts have taken three principal forms. First, long-standing regional disputes; second, short-lived military hostilities; finally, localized disputes. Inter-state conflict has included Arab against Iranian, Israeli against Arab, and Arab versus Arab. Regional conflict has been primarily in the context of the Arab–Israeli dispute, while conflict between regional players and outside actors is typified by the Suez crisis of 1956. In the same category the Kuwait crisis uniquely brought together an alliance between local and outside powers confronting an Arab aggressor. Internal state conflict and sectarian violence is epitomized by our case study on the Lebanon devastated by fifteen years of civil war from 1975–1990. We have also looked at the tragic case of the Kurds – a people scattered throughout several countries in the region who have failed to achieve any acceptable degree of self-determination and whose struggle for the recognition of their legitimate political rights seems almost hopeless.

Previous treatments of conflicts in the region have examined such factors as traditional state-to-state rivalries and competition for control of natural resources such as oil or water. It was only in the 1990s, in the wake of the Cold War and following the end of superpower rivalry, that historical accounts of conflict in the region addressed new issues. These included ethno-national rivalry and the impact of continued foreign interference in the region in supporting a variety of corrupt and authoritarian regimes. In addition, debates in the 1990s began to focus increasingly on the issue of regime legitimacy and a linkage to continuing conflicts. In some cases, like that of Iraq, people questioned the morality of allowing authoritarian leaders like Saddam Hussein to 'engineer' national crises through provoking conflict in order to entrench his autocratic system of rule, although he was far from alone in doing so. The validity of the arguments put forward by both the former Soviet Union and the United States in defence of their roles in the region has also been questioned in an era where the US's foothold in much of the area has largely been the target of popular resentment; in contrast with the less critical attitude of those regimes dependent on Washington for support and protection.

This book does not include a chapter specifically about the military and its role in the Middle East. But the predominance of the armed forces in much of the politics of the region, their role in the nature and process of state formation and nation building, needs to be understood in the context of the wider debate about conflict. Since 1945 there have been major wars between Israel and the Arabs, as well as the Iran–Iraq war and the Gulf crisis of 1990 to 1991. In addition there have been civil conflicts in Iraq, Syria, Algeria, Jordan, Yemen and Lebanon in which the armed forces of these states have played a major role. Such wars have been described by Bromley as 'the main source of conflict in the Middle East', and are, 'concerned with the internal pacification and repression of domestic populations'.[2]

A further reflection of the ill-defined nature of the state in the region has been the numerous border disputes which have erupted over the years. They have included conflicts between Egypt and Libya, Morocco and Mauritania, Jordan and Syria, Israel and Lebanon, Iraq and Kuwait, Iran and Iraq, Saudi Arabia and Yemen, Bahrain and Qatar. Much of this conflict is the legacy of colonial-inspired or crafted state formation from the turn of the twentieth century to the 1970s. The carve-up of much of the Middle East was determined by the strategic objectives of the former colonial powers – principally Britain and France – who created highly artificial states, many of whose borders remain subject to dispute. Such strategic objectives were largely pursued with no consideration for the interests or wishes of the indigenous peoples of the region; the same people who were obliged to live within the boundaries of new, highly artificial states which they themselves had taken no part in shaping. In many contemporary accounts of origins of war in the region such factors are often forgotten. But the terrible (if unforeseen) consequences of colonial ambitions are not forgotten by many in the region who still perceive Arthur Balfour and the British as the architects of conflicts which continue to the present day.[3]

The arms race in the region has also played its part in perpetuating conflict. Arab states, Iran and Israel all spent the latter half of the twentieth century building up significant arsenals, including conventional weaponry, chemical weapons and, certainly in Israel's case, nuclear capability – thus the real fear, particularly in the 1970s, of a nuclear Armageddon in the area.

Western and Soviet support for the arms race has been ill disguised and has been used to further vital economic and or strategic interests within the region. National spending on arms and the military in the region is higher than other developing regions in the world. While in the Middle East spending on arms and the military is cited on average as 15 per cent of national income it is only 5 per cent in the rest of the developing world.[4] In Syria, for example, defence expenditure is as high as 18 per cent, and the army constitutes 3.9 per cent of the total workforce compared to 0.8 per cent in the United States.[5]

In such an arena of conflict awash with arms, the role of the military in the political systems of the area can scarcely be exaggerated. Military coups and revolutions have been a significant feature of the Middle East and military-based regimes characteristic of states such as Iraq, Syria, Libya and Egypt. As part of this phenomenon, or because of it, the emergence of the soldier politician linked to the militaristic nature of the state in the region has a direct cause-and-effect relationship on the political processes of countries like Syria, Turkey, Libya and Iraq. This is the case even in democratic Israel where the military record of its soldier-politicians, including Prime Ministers like Yitzhak Rabin and Ehud Barak, are promoted (and admired) as positive attributes of a national leader.

The domination of military rule over national political systems, however, is not of course unique to the Middle East and remains a feature of many Third World regimes all over the globe. Indeed, in the 1960s, the role of the military in the politics of the region was perceived as a positive development heralding progress, technological advancement, modernization, and the promotion and safeguarding of an appropriate nationalist agenda. A dramatic volte-face in popular attitudes occurred two decades later. The true nature of conflict and the military in society had convinced many that the negative effects of this feature of politics in the region was unacceptable:

> The pervasive nature of factionalism and internal strife within the officer class, the lack of economic development, economic crises, widespread corruption, coercion and lack of democracy convinced many that . . . whatever degree of order and discipline the military have been able to provide, it has been outweighed by the blocking of the assumption of responsibility on the part of ordinary citizens for their economic and political affairs'.[6]

In addition, the closing decades of the twentieth century witnessed a steady transition from military to civil rule elsewhere in the world. But despite this sea change in popular sentiment this did not happen in the Middle East where, as Halliday comments, 'relations between states are dominated by suspicion, a stance reinforced by popular attitudes on all sides where memories of recent war remain strong'.[7]

While the role of the military and conflict has been debated extensively in many texts on the subject, other explanations of conflict also need to be highlighted. Conflicting ideologies, ethnic and religious differences, super-power rivalry and the development of state nationalism are all factors that have been cited to one degree or another in explanation of conflict in the region. All these factors are examined in the case studies we have selected for treatment in this volume. There are obvious omissions, such as the troubles of Sudan or Morocco, hostilities in the Horn of Africa, Britain's withdrawal from South Yemen and other bloody colonial disengagements such as by the French in North Africa. In such a short volume we have had to leave some of the regional conflicts to one side, but we hope that the themes we highlight in discussing some will go some way in shedding light on most of the others.

Finally we have laid out the book as follows. In the first two chapters we examine two important dimensions of the Arab–Israeli conflict. We disentangle the narrower Palestinian–Israeli dimension from wider disputes between the state of Israel and the Arab states of the region. Some might argue that to treat the conflict in this way does a disservice to the much-vaunted principle of solidarity and unity sought by the Arab people in its confrontation with Israel. We, however, are not arguing that separate treatment necessitates a separation of the unifying principles at the heart of such struggles. Rather, we take a pragmatic approach to assist the first-time reader in understanding the roots of such conflicts while reflecting, as we do in both chapters, on the linkages within the dispute.

In Chapter 3 we examine the impact of the Soviet Union and the United States in the region, as well as superpower rivalry and its influence on the course of conflict and peacemaking from the 1950s onwards. No account of conflict in the region since 1945 can afford to dismiss the role played by such actors and the impact the cold war had on both hindering the resolution of conflict and actively promoting it to satisfy superpower strategic objectives. In Chapter 4 we address the dominant perception in the West that in the latter decades of the twentieth century Islam has been a primary catalyst for conflict and a major threat emanating from the region. We aim to debunk much of the reductive rhetoric associated with this perception and put so-called 'Holy Terror' in its proper perspective.

In Chapter 5 we look at manifestations of the religious nature of conflict in the region through the examination of the causes of the civil war in Lebanon and how it fitted into the larger jigsaw of the Arab–Israeli dispute and superpower politics. Further ethnic dimensions of conflict are explored in the following chapter on the Kurds, where we chart the rise of ethno-nationalism in the context of uniting ideologies of nationalism and the challenges presented by minority groups agitating for their rights, including that of self-determination.

A clash of ideologies of sorts is explained in Chapter 7 when we discuss the nature of the war between Iran and Iraq, which dominated the Gulf throughout the 1980s. Described by one writer as a 'meaningless' conflict with uncountable costs, we examine the political motives that brought these neighbouring states into major confrontation and the destabilizing impact this had throughout the Gulf region. The battle for local hegemony and a desperate scramble for resources, also in the Gulf, are identified in Chapter 8 as the main factors in explaining Saddam Hussein's disastrous invasion of Kuwait in August 1990 and his subsequent defeat at the hands of the Desert Storm coalition.

In Chapter 9 we describe how the nature of conflict in the region was changed by a variety of concerted attempts in the 1990s to bring them to an end. In Lebanon, for example, where significant civil conflict had gripped the country since 1975, an Arab-sponsored deal brought the conflict to a halt and allowed the country to begin a return to parliamentary politics. While the root causes of the conflict in Lebanon remain unresolved, there is hope that appropriate scenarios can be designed to satisfy the more pressing demands of the various factions in this state. Elsewhere in the region, other Arab attempts at conflict resolution have been marginalized, and it has only been the influence of outside agencies, especially the United States, that has brought formerly intractable enemies to the negotiating table. These recent developments have the potential to significantly alter the political landscape of the region, but comprehensive peace remains an elusive prospect.

Our last chapter is a new one, bringing the story up to date following the dramatic events of 11 September 2001. As described in the Preface, this horrendous event cast its shadow on the then virtually stalled Middle East Peace Process (MEPP), led to regime change in Afghanistan and, as part of President Bush's wider war on terrorism, started the countdown to the US-led invasion of Iraq in March 2003, Iraq having been categorized by the US President as target number one within the 'axis of evil'. Its ramifications will be with us for many years, as the quick coalition victory liberating Iraq (or at least putting the Saddam regime to flight) seems to have been the easy bit. Nation rebuilding in this traumatized and divided country will be a major headache for the international community and, more immediately, for the coalition partners cast as much in the role of occupiers as of liberators. We also look at the prospects for reactivating the MEPP in the light of the launching of the 'road map' – a blueprint for a lasting and comprehensive solution to this (nearly) sixty years' war. Even cautious optimism may be premature, despite President Bush's apparent determination to emulate his predecessor's personal engagement, the process has got off to an uncertain start amidst a new welter of bloodshed. As in Iraq, the international community faces an uphill task.

1   The Arab–Israeli conflict
Ways of war

It is not true that the Arabs hate the Jews for personal, religious, or racial reasons. They see us, rightly from their point of view, as Westerners, foreigners, even invaders who seized an Arab country to create a Jewish state ... Since we are obliged to achieve our aims against the wishes of the Arabs, we must live in a permanent war.

General Moshe Dayan[1]

For the best part of a century the Arab–Israeli conflict has been a complex problem with important ramifications for the international community. As other chapters in this book will highlight, this conflict has embroiled other actors such as the USA and the former Soviet Union into, on one occasion, near nuclear confrontation. It has had a major impact on the international and more specifically capital-based economies of the international order, and promoted extravagant, wasteful and profligate spending on arms to the point where Kalashnikovs are apparently more valued by many of the region's political leaders than a decent standard of living for its citizens. How then does one begin to make sense of this bitter feud between the Jews and the Arabs, the state of Israel and the Arab and other states of the region, between religious cousins and territorial neighbours? In our first two chapters we aim to analyse this problem by making a distinction on the one hand between the wider Arab–Israeli conflict – marked by the wars of 1948, 1967, 1973, 1982, the peace treaties of 1978 between Israel and Egypt, and 1994 between Jordan and Israel – and on the other the more narrowly focused Palestinian Israeli dispute that resulted in the Arab revolt of 1936 to 1939, the wars cited above and the outbreak of the Palestinian Uprising (Intifada) in 1987, as well as attempts at peacemaking between the two parties from 1993 onwards.

Some might argue that making such distinctions is unhelpful; after all should we not liken the conflict to the chicken-and-egg conundrum, asking

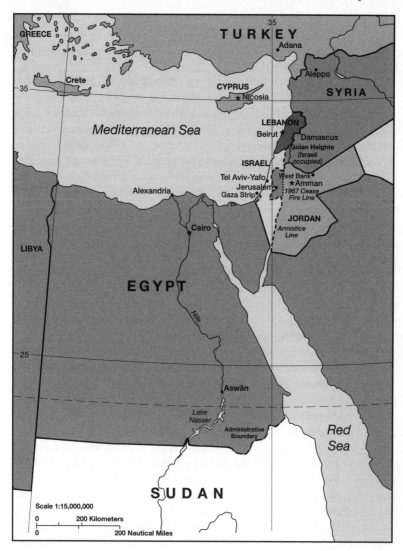

Map B – Israel and neighbouring states

which came first, the Arab–Israeli dispute or the Palestinian–Israeli? Such riddles rarely have a simple answer, which is why we believe it is best to try and make distinctions between the two in order to assist understanding rather than to obscure or confuse. It is true, of course, that the Palestinian issue lies at the heart of the wider conflict. We will argue, however, that the importance of the Palestinians as the primary focus has waxed and waned over the past century and that other factors, such as the competition between rival Arab states for regional leadership, need to be explained if this conflict is to be adequately understood.

The conflict between those regularly referred to as the Jews and the Arabs has been well under way for nearly a century. While major military confrontation between Israel and its Arab neighbours has not occurred since the Israeli invasion of Lebanon in 1982, the absence of meaningful peace and the maintenance of conflict continued to the end of the century. Within its confines the differences between these peoples, religions and attitudes have at times manifested themselves in conventional wars, and led to the militarization of the entire region, where even aspiring democrats have only recently begun to discard their military uniforms. Inevitably under such a climate, economic relations, culture, history, literature, mass media and communications, international organizations, regional associations and interest groups have all been enlisted and manipulated to demonize the enemy. Rival nationalisms, the superpower conflict, the right to self-determination, anti-Semitism, control of oil, and the emergence of the Third World radicalism and anti-Western sentiment have all played their part, making up the cocktail of conflict described by Sahliyeh as 'the most lethal and volatile . . . and the most difficult to resolve'.[2]

Although the essence of the conflict is the battle between two people over one land, the territory of the Holy Land including Jerusalem, over time the Arab–Israeli dimension has developed characteristics often far-removed from the original Palestinian issue and territorial focus. One example is the bitter dispute and battle that has raged from the late 1970s between Israel and the Lebanese Islamic resistance movements, and latterly the Shi'a Hizballah organization. While Israel's original motives in invading and subsequently occupying Lebanon in 1978 and 1982 were to rout the PLO, once the PLO had left the country the Israeli Defence Force (IDF) remained as an occupying force and made themselves the principal enemies of the Lebanese Shi'a population.[3] Hizballah was subsequently formed as a resistance movement to end Israel's illegal occupation of southern Lebanon and, until Israel's withdrawal in spring 2000, waged a major military campaign against its enemy and those perceived to be its supporters. While it may be true that there was little love lost between the PLO and Hizballah during the Lebanese civil war they ended up sharing a common antipathy to Israel as an occupying force on Arab lands. Certainly this is an instance where Israel's policies may have inadvertently created allies out of enemies, thus undermining the security of their own state.

The roots of this conflict lay in the resistance mounted by the Arabs and their leaders in the region against the initial attempt by settler Zionists, most of whom were immigrants from Europe, to build a state in Palestine. But it was the subsequent dispossession of the Palestinian Arab population, the creation of a Palestinian national identity and the emergence of new Arab nationalisms united in opposition to Zionism and to the close association it was perceived as having with the forces of imperialism and colonialism, which gave the conflict its wider dimension. The struggle to gain and retain Arab rights to self-determination over Palestine in the face of European dominance over the entire region had its roots in the First World War, when the British made contradictory commitments to the Arabs and to the Zionist Jews to enlist their support against Germany and its Ottoman (Turkish) allies. The Arab leadership was led to believe that Arabs would control much of the region following the defeat of the Ottomans. But at the same time the British and the French were planning to replace Istanbul as the dominant power in the region. The situation was complicated further by a British promise to the Zionists to support the establishment of a Jewish national home in Arab Palestine: the Balfour Declaration, which is described in Chapter 2. The expediency of measures taken to further war aims was to be questioned in the decades that followed. It soon emerged that the British had promised more than they could deliver and had engaged in what later emerged as duplicitous behaviour described as a 'disgusting scramble for the Middle East'.[4]

When the Ottoman Empire was dissolved at the end of the First World War most of the Middle East became subject to colonial rule or influence. European powers, principally Britain and France, re-drew the boundaries of the Middle East and many Arab areas came under their direct political control. This period of direct and indirect colonial control, short lived though it was, resulted in the invention and promotion of new Arab rulers and monarchs presiding over newly created states within artificial boundaries. It sowed the seeds of future conflicts – between Israel and the Arabs (involving the Iranians) and amongst the Arabs themselves – that for the most part remained unresolved throughout the last century.

As we describe in the next chapter, the incipient conflict between the Jews and Arabs in the region took shape during the first three decades of the twentieth century and culminated in the first direct war in 1948 as Britain ended its mandate in Palestine, which had lasted from 1919 to 1948. During this period the British authorities were, according to the official remit of the mandate as agreed by the League of Nations, supposed to assist the mandated territory to self-government. But they were caught between conflicting pressures: Zionist attempts to establish their own state (something more than the 'National Home' envisaged in the Balfour Declaration, as incorporated into the mandate's provisions) and Arab efforts to oppose this in the pursuit of their own national aspirations.[5] In these circumstances the

British had little option but to pursue an often oppressive policy of control and public order.

The perceived grievances of the Palestinian community in Palestine at the time (particularly the large influx of Jewish immigrants) raised tension between the two communities and resulted in the 1929 riots when Jews in Jerusalem and Hebron were murdered. This event was followed by further conflict including the 1936 General Strike and the Palestinian revolt from 1936 to 1939. The British authorities, also under attack from militant Jewish organizations, appeared to be unable to develop policies or strategies to resolve the conflict, and the outbreak of the Second World War in Europe in 1939, and the Nazi-perpetrated Holocaust against 6 million Jews, had unforeseen consequences for the future of Palestine. After the Second World War Jewish immigration reached new heights, and pressure for a Jewish state in Palestine as a haven for the persecuted survivors of the Holocaust grew relentlessly. The British were increasingly unable to maintain law and order, and meanwhile the Palestinians and their national leadership demanded self-determination. Eventually the whole problem was turned over by the British to the newly established United Nations, who decided to resolve the competing claims for self-determination by promoting partition between the Jews and the Arabs, with Jerusalem falling under international authority. The Zionist movement accepted statehood as a much better deal than the 'national home' they had been offered under the Balfour Declaration. They already faced considerable hostility and incipient conflict from their Arab neighbours. There was a belief that securing statehood would promote the much-needed sense of security for the Jewish people and an end to their exile. The diaspora could be gathered in under the flag of Israel. However, the Palestinians and Arab states rejected the UN partition plan, arguing that it was inherently biased and ignored the legitimate rights of Palestinians. The Palestinians complained that their land was being given away as a means of appeasing European guilt over the Holocaust. When the British withdrew in May 1948 the battle for the land of Palestine broke out in earnest between the Israelis and the Arabs.

The war broke out shortly after the Israeli Declaration of Independence on 15 May 1948, as units from the Arab armies of Egypt, Jordan and Syria (backed by forces from Lebanon and Iraq) attempted to win back the Palestinian soil that had been lost to the Israeli state. The Arab armies, poorly led and equipped, were ultimately unsuccessful and failed to defeat the small but well-motivated and highly trained Israeli Defence Force. The armistice negotiations did not occur until January 1949, by which time between 700,000 and 800,000 Palestinians had fled their homes or been forced to flee. In some cases Palestinians, encouraged by their Arab leaders, left the battle-zones in the belief that after a swift Arab victory they would be able to return. In other cases Palestinians fled their villages after hearing news of the massacre by Israeli forces in the village of Deir Yassin. As Rodinson notes, 'Many leading Jews were glad to see the departure of a population which by its very presence presented an obstacle to the realisation of the Jewish state projected by the Zionists.'[6] The Palestinians who arrived as refugees in Lebanon, Transjordan, Syria, Egypt and the Gaza Strip quickly realized that they had lost their homes and would not be allowed to return to them. The only comfort that the leaders of the Arab world could offer was the promise that this first encounter was just one war in a major conflict that would continue on their behalf. The Palestinian community refers to this period in their history as '*al-nakbah*' – the catastrophe.

In terms of territory the end of the war meant the effective partition of Palestine as it was formerly known. The West Bank and East Jerusalem (including the old city) came under the control of Jordan and its monarch King Abdullah. The Egyptian government administered the Gaza Strip from Cairo. The rest of the country, which as a result of the armistice had enlarged from 14,000 to 21,000 square kilometres, came within the new Israeli state. The Arabs were thus left with one-fifth of the original territory of their land and their aspirations for an Arab Palestine battered and weakened by the war.

Thus, within hours of its birth the new Israeli state had been compelled into war with its Arab neighbours. The war lasted until armistice agreements secured in January 1949. Aware of their poor chances, the intertwined political and military leadership of Israel had no option but to engage in the fight against the six Arab armies ranged against them. One advantage that the Israelis believed they had over their enemy was referred to by Israeli Chief of Operations Yigael Yadin in May 1948 when he remarked, 'the problem is to what extent our men will be able to overcome enemy forces by virtue of their fighting spirit, of our planning and our tactics'.[7] The new state, forged in war, emerged from that experience with a unique character and an emphasis on institutions, such as the military, which might not, under more peaceful circumstances of statehood, have been necessary.

The repercussions of the conflict were widespread and enduring. Amongst them was an initial period of instability in the Arab countries as they came to terms with their defeat, and a backlash against British and Western influence in the region. This was most noticeable in increasing popular opposition to the British-supported Hashemite monarchies in Iraq and in Jordan. In 1951 Jordan's King Abdullah was assassinated and the new King Hussein – bowing to popular pressure – dismissed General Glubb Pasha, the British commander of the Arab Legion. The upsurge of popular nationalism elsewhere across the region in response to the Arab defeat signalled the end of the corrupt royalist regime in Egypt, where, in 1952, the

Free Officer Movement led by Gamal Abdel Nasser mounted a coup, trumpeting the rhetoric of Arab nationalism and unity in the face of the Zionist enemy across the region. In the eyes of Arab nationalist radicals in Cairo, Beirut, Baghdad and Damascus, Israel was an enemy not just because of the injustice against their brethren in Palestine but also because of its close association with what they perceived as Western imperialist aspirations towards the region and in particular its recently exploited massive oil reserves. Thus, radical Arab nationalism and pan-Arab pretensions created a new dimension in the conflict with Israel, as was strikingly demonstrated during the 1956 Suez war.

The Suez conflict, which erupted over the decision by Nasser to nationalize the Suez Canal Company in July 1956, was a major escalation of anti-colonialist and, by association, anti-Zionist sentiment in the Arab world. The Suez Canal was built in the 1860s and by the late 1880s came under British and other foreign control (via a number of shareholders), maintained by British occupation of Egypt. The British saw the canal as an essential element in their control of the main sea route to India. In the four-year period leading up to the nationalization of the Suez Canal, Nasser embarked on a programme of pan-Arab cohesion and made military pacts with Syria, Saudi Arabia and Yemen. Nasser's goal was the restoration of the Arab nation under Egyptian leadership and an end to foreign influence in the area. The nationalization of Suez was the first time that a Third World country had successfully regained one of its major foreign-owned assets.

Both the French and the British were outraged at Nasser's decision. A highly secret tripartite operation in collusion with the Israelis was organized. They hatched a plot to regain control over the Suez Canal. On 29 October 1956 the Israeli army launched Operation Kadesch; their forces crossed the border and entered the Sinai desert. Over a period of five days they routed the Egyptian army and approached the canal. In accordance with a pre-arranged plan – 'Operation Musketeer' – the British and French bombed Egyptian targets and sent their troops to occupy Port Said and Port Fuad on the pretext of protecting them from hostile action, whether from Israel or Egypt. The Israelis had accepted a ceasefire as part of the secret pre-arrangement with the British and French, but the Egyptians refused to pull their troops back from the canal. Despite the military successes, the British and French were forced to accept a ceasefire and withdraw their forces as a result of US economic pressure on Britain and international public opinion as expressed through the UN. Nasser had held on to the canal and Arab nationalist feelings and anti-imperialist sentiment reached an all-time high.

The dispute between the Arabs and Israelis was exacerbated by the Arab perception of the Israeli role in the conflict as nothing more than defender of Western interests in the region. As a result tensions remained high and the deep animosity between the nations worsened. By siding with France and Britain and continuing to occupy the Gaza Strip between 1956 and 1957, the Israelis managed not only to further deepen the rift with Egypt but also to anger the USA, bringing a close relationship under severe pressure. Within Israel the involvement of their armed forces in the 1956 crisis was perceived quite differently. The Israeli political and military establishment were concerned by persistent Arab attacks on Israel mounted from Gaza and the Sinai and by the Egyptian blockade of the Red Sea; consequently, the Israeli port of Eilat took defensive steps against Egyptian belligerence. While it is true that the Israeli withdrawal from the Sinai in March 1957 was prompted by US and UN pressure, Israeli involvement in Suez, secret agreements apart, would have been considered part of the domestic security strategy and sold as such to the Israeli people. In many respects the legacy of 1956 would not be visited upon the Israelis for some ten years or more. There can be little doubt, however, that Nasser's motives in 1967 were, at least partially, rooted in the 1956 encounter and his memories of military humiliation.

The war of 1967 was inevitable; the disputes between the Arabs and the Israelis had remained unresolved and the era of fervent and self-confident Arab nationalism was at its peak. On the eve of the war the combined Arab troop numbers were more than double those of the Israelis. The Arabs also had three times as many tanks and aircraft, yet within six days they were totally routed by the Israeli army. The build up to the war on the Arab side had been fraught with reckless rhetoric and strident propaganda about the military prowess of the 'Arab people' and their ability to defeat the Israelis, to sweep them into the sea and win back Palestine. Egypt was the most eager of the combatants and was in a sense a victim of its own propaganda, which grossly exaggerated its potential as a military power. The Syrians and Jordanians, with territory at stake, were somewhat less hawkish but came under pressure from Nasser and the weight of their own public opinion intoxicated by the prospect of victory.[8] Nasser, determined to earn his place in the history books as the undisputed leader of the Arab world, pursued the liberation of Palestine as if it were a Holy Grail. At the same time he oppressed the Egyptian-administered Palestinian population of the Gaza Strip and the refugee community in Egypt, imprisoning thousands of them throughout his presidency.

The war was over in a matter of five or six days between 5 and 11 June. The Jordanian army was defeated and its airforce destroyed; similar Israeli victories occurred over the Egyptians in the Gaza Strip and the Syrians in the Golan Heights. By Saturday 10 June 1967 the Israeli army occupied the Sinai Peninsula, the Gaza Strip, the West Bank (including East Jerusalem and the old city) and the Golan Heights. The acquisition of territory by the end of the war had increased Israel's size by six times (almost half that formerly administered by Jordan), and this had massive logistical, military and political implications for the Israeli government.

The role of the UN during the hostilities was minimal. However, on 22 November after five months of bargaining, the UN passed SCR 242 which required a withdrawal of Israeli forces from the territories occupied in exchange for the cessation of fighting, the recognition of all states in the region, freedom of navigation in the Suez Canal and in the Gulf of Aqaba, and the creation of demilitarized zones.[9] Once again Israel was able to prevail militarily despite the odds stacked against it. Following the appointment of Moshe Dayan as Defence Minister just days before the war, the Israeli armed forces meticulously planned their daring campaign against a belligerent Nasser and his Egyptian forces. By seizing the initiative, launching the war before the Arabs got there first, the Israelis were able to dominate the rest of the military campaign, first by air and then by land. By the end of the war, Israel, a 'country that had felt embattled and threatened only days before was now the decisive military power in the Middle East . . . Equally Israel had changed in the process, for she was now an occupying power.'[10]

The fourth conflict between Israel and the Arabs in twenty-five years since 1948 had a number of unique features. First, Egyptian and Syrian forces were able (albeit temporarily) to break through Israeli lines, an unprecedented military success for the Arabs. Second, although Israel was the ultimate victor, the perceived weakness of the army in the initial stages of the hostilities affected national morale and self-confidence and led political leaders to rethink their position vis-à-vis their Arab neighbours. Third, the war was an Egyptian and Syrian attempt to recover their own territory, with the Palestinian issue coming a poor second in terms of strategy and objectives. Finally, it was during this war that the Gulf States started to use oil prices and boycott as major weapons against the West. For the first time the West was made aware of the significant leverage the Arab states held over the oil-dependent economies of the capitalist world.

In 1973 Nasser's successor, President Anwar Sadat, announced that he was preparing to attack Israel in an attempt to recover territory lost in the war of 1967. Sadat had been making such statements for a number of years while conducting a low-key campaign of attrition across the canal, so such announcements were not treated seriously. But although both American and Israeli intelligence networks were to a great extent aware of the plans, little was done in preparation for an attack. Nevertheless, on 6 October, the Egyptians crossed Suez and the Syrians attacked the Golan Heights. The US and the Russians immediately commenced a diplomatic effort to halt the conflict. At this point, as we discuss further in Chapter 3, neither of the superpowers wanted to risk being drawn into the conflict. By the second week of the war the situation began to turn in Israel's favour, reversing earlier Syrian and Egyptian gains. By 24 October Israeli tanks had reached the suburbs of Cairo.

At the last minute the Americans began to pressurize the Israelis, and Sadat went to the UN for a ceasefire agreement. The UN passed resolution 338 calling for the ceasefire. By 24 October the fighting had stopped. The Israelis had ultimately been successful, but the war demonstrated that they now had to regard Arab forces – especially the Egyptians – as being a match for their own and that the conflict would inevitably continue.

While the superpowers had been able to impose a ceasefire agreement, arranging an enduring peace was shown to be a difficult and lengthy process. One outcome of the war was that the US administration was forced to make a serious effort to push for peace between Israel and the Arab states. The war had exacerbated the instability of an already unstable Middle East, had frustrated American ambitions in the region, and hit the US economy through the oil embargo announced by Arab oil producers. An OPEC (Organization of Petroleum Exporting Countries) increase in oil prices of several hundred per cent, plus the total embargo against the US announced by Saudi Arabia and other Arab oil producers on 19 October, was intended to achieve a number of goals, with the resolution of the Palestinian issue among them. As Gerner notes, 'analysts differ on whether the events of 1973 resulted in a fundamental restructuring of the relationship between the Arab oil-producing countries and the West'.[11] It seems likely that it did.

At Camp David – the summer residence of the US President – on 17 September 1978 President Carter succeeded in getting the leaders of Egypt and Israel to sign a peace treaty between their two countries and agree to a framework of negotiation for peace in the Middle East. The achievement of the peace between Israel and Egypt was a momentous event in the history of the Arab–Israeli dispute. After the 1973 war Sadat felt he had little to lose in 'throwing in his lot' with the US. He knew that in terms of diplomatic settlement only the US could deliver Israel into a peace, for they alone had enough influence over the Israelis to prise concessions out of them. He was also hopeful that a programme of US economic assistance would benefit the Egyptian economy.

For Sadat, initially, one important aspect of the treaty was the opportunity to link the Egyptian–Israeli peace to the issue of the Palestinians. However, the Egyptian domestic situation, especially economic pressures, made Sadat desperate to reach an agreement even in the face of minimal Israeli concessions. The Palestinians were suspicious of Sadat's role and reluctant to be associated with an agreement negotiated in their absence. This resulted in the issue of the Palestinians becoming sidelined in the peace negotiations as being too difficult. Sadat paid a high price for his willingness to make peace with the government of Israel and it ultimately led to his assassination on 6 October 1981. The peace treaty also left Egypt isolated in the Arab world, declared a pariah and shunned by the other Arab states.

The Egyptian–Israeli peace treaty was the product of intense negotiations, accompanied by theatrical grandstanding, influenced by an array of economic inducements and domestic pressures and achieved through the success of the American government in bringing the two parties together. It demonstrated that Washington had the ability to influence Israel when its interests demanded it. It has been argued that the treaty was purely the result of US pressure for settlement of the Arab–Israeli conflict (which among other things was destabilizing world oil prices). Certainly the American role at this stage of the peace process could accurately be described as dominating and exclusive. Attempts by Sadat in 1976 to get the UN to resolve to internationalize the peace conference were thwarted by the US, a policy that Washington has tended to follow ever since. Carter recognized the importance of the Palestinian issue as central to the resolution of the Arab–Israeli conflict. A separate peace would flounder if Palestine was not dealt with, and Camp David proved him right. To a certain degree US influence in the peace process meant that it was able to establish a new foothold in the Middle East whilst enhancing its special relationship with Israel. However, this was the limit of American achievement. It had been hoped that the peace process would encourage other Arab states like Iraq, Jordan and Syria to enter into a similar process. Instead these states joined the Soviet-sponsored radical 'Rejectionist' front headed by Syria who aimed the majority of their attacks at American 'Imperialist and Zionist' policies.

The Israelis, for their part, viewed the treaty as a success. Although they had succumbed to some extent to US pressure in making peace with Egypt on terms Cairo could accept, overall they had gained much and conceded little (a return of the Sinai). They had also effectively neutralized the one Arab power that presented a significant military threat to their security. The adage 'No war without Egypt' accurately applied here. In addition, by pursuing a bilateral peace treaty they adroitly avoided linkage to the Palestinian issue. Egypt regained the Sinai, lost the respect of the rest of the Arab world and was regarded as an outcast. The Palestinians gained nothing from the peace treaty – not that they had sought anything. The Israelis promised unspecific long-term considerations for granting Palestinian autonomy. In the meantime Israeli concerns focused on the Palestinian threat both within and outside their borders; more specifically the escalation of fedayeen attacks from the southern area of Lebanon then termed 'Fatahland'.

In this context it was no surprise that the Israeli Prime Minister Begin made no secret of the fact that as far as he was concerned a peace agreement with Egypt would ignore the Palestinian right to self-determination.

Menachim Begin's decision to invade Lebanon was in some senses an Israeli answer to the Palestinian issue but ultimately embroiled others further in the conflict and put the usually cordial US–Israeli relationship under severe pressure. Israeli logic behind the invasion was twofold. First, to protect its northern borders from Lebanon-based Palestinian guerrilla attacks; second, to expel the PLO from Lebanon. Aware that Sadat's only concern was not to compromise regaining the Sinai, that the Arab world was divided and the PLO relatively isolated, Israeli leaders felt they had a free hand to sort out Lebanon for themselves. In 1978 they had already briefly invaded the country, establishing what was referred to as a 'buffer zone' in Lebanon's southern territory. They had been forced to retreat as a result of US pressure.

Throughout 1981 there was a noticeable rise in tension: a missile crisis with Syria in spring was followed on 7 June by the raid against the Iraqi nuclear centre of Tammuz. By December Israel had formally annexed the Golan Heights, which had been captured from the Syrians in the war of 1967. But, crucially, in June 1981 the IDF and PLO troops based in south Lebanon began shelling each other until the United States negotiated a ceasefire with the two parties. Against this background, it was inevitable that certain elements of the Israeli military would use their influence within government to take action against the PLO in Lebanon. Although there were splits within the military over this issue, the 'hawks' prevailed and steered Begin into a further course of invasion.

'Peace for Galilee' was the name given to the Israeli invasion of Lebanon in June 1982. Officially the Israelis declared that their march across the border was only a question of affirming control of a 40 km strip, from which terrorists would no longer be able to shell the north of the country. Yet, despite these apparently limited aims, the IDF soon found itself in Beirut. The city was soon under Israeli imposed blockade. Thus began the siege of mainly Muslim and Palestinian West Beirut, where Palestinians and the Lebanese National Movement fought side by side, whilst the Christian Phalangists lent support to the IDF as it attempted to eradicate the PLO. There seemed no end to the phosphorous, napalm, scatter, and imploding bombs that relentlessly poured down on the starving, parched west section of the city. Apart from 6,000 PLO guerrillas in the besieged city, there were some half a million Lebanese and Palestinian civilians, and every day of the bombardment about 200 or 300 of them were killed.

As the bombardment went on, day after day, the international community looked on impotently, seemingly mesmerized by the brutal nature of the

Israeli action. The European Economic Community (EEC), the UN Security Council and other bodies issued condemnations, while the United States remonstrated ineffectually with its protégé and was brusquely snubbed. Yet it is difficult to disagree with Gilmour's conclusion that

> the most feeble reaction came from the Arab world which seemed petrified into silence and inaction. Beirut, the ideological birthplace of Arab nationalism and for long the intellectual and commercial capital of the Arab world, was being pulverised by a brutal foreign army while the Arab states did nothing.[12]

In this respect Israel succeeded in its greatest victory in its conflict with the Arab world, and exposed the hollow posturing of the grand slogans of 'Arab unity' in the face of the Zionist threat. If the leaders of the Arab world could not rally to the defence of its brethren in Beirut as Israeli tanks rolled into its suburbs, what did unity mean?

On 30 August 1982 the PLO admitted defeat and the leadership and guerrillas left Lebanon in shame. Arafat moved on to Tunis and the PLO network went with him. The departure of the PLO, however, was not the end of Israel's battle against the Palestinians of Lebanon. On 16 and 17 September Israeli troops moved into West Beirut, and their Phalangist allies massacred at least 2,000 children, women and elderly men in the refugee camps of Sabra and Shatilla. Israeli collusion in the massacres appalled the world.

Such was the tragic end of the first phase of the Lebanon war. A second phase now began: that of Israel's occupation of southern Lebanon, which came to a humiliating end for them in May 2000 when Hizballah resistance fighters hastened the retreat of the Israeli army, which by then had suffered heavy casualties and brought about the collapse of Israel's local ally, the South Lebanon Army (SLA).[13] For eighteen years Israel remained in Lebanon and promoted its presence through its local ally, the Christian-led SLA. United Nations forces, mandated in 1978 to act as peacekeepers until Israel withdrew, found themselves embroiled in various battles between Lebanon's militias and the SLA and IDF. Israel's northern border remained vulnerable to attack and domestic pressure grew for an end to Israel's Lebanon experience. As Israeli casualty rates rose the country's political leaders responded. In 1999, following his election as Prime Minister, former Defence Chief Ehud Barak announced that Israeli troops would finally be withdrawn from Lebanon.

As this chapter has demonstrated, there are no outright winners and far too many losers in this brief balance sheet of the Arab–Israeli conflict. During the course of these hostilities national revenues have been squandered on the purchase of weapons. Some states have further impoverished themselves in seeking loans from Western arms manufacturers and governments to purchase a technology dedicated to regional domination rather than development. In as much as the Palestinian issue has closed Arab ranks in the quest for justice it has perhaps also done as much to divide the Arab world, ordinary citizens and leaders alike.

Progress towards resolving the dispute seems to have only been achieved under two significant conditions. The first is American pressure, influence and guarantees in winning concessions from Israel and rewarding the parties involved (financially) for taking risks on peace. The second is the Israeli-preferred route of negotiation via bilateral rather than multi-lateral or international forums such as the United Nations. Washington, generally speaking, has supported this tactic and facilitated such a process at Camp David in the negotiation of a separate peace between Israel and Egypt. For those who still believe that the only way a just and comprehensive peace can be forged in the Middle East is through the participation of the international community and the UN there can be little cause for comfort in achievements so far. But, however reached, a lasting and just peace depends not on treaties forged by outside parties able to cajole and pressure leaders but in the quality of that peace and its sustainability through popular acceptance over present and future generations in both Israel and the Arab world.

2   The Palestinian–Israeli conflict
Hostages to history

Some of the most enduring images of the twentieth century have been generated by the Palestinian–Israeli conflict. The historic handshake in September 1993 between Israeli leader Yitzhak Rabin and Palestinian chief Yasser Arafat is but one of them. For the better part of a century the conflict of two peoples over one land has defined the politics of the region and has had a major impact on many aspects of international politics, including the cold war, political economy, and international and state terrorism. In some respects, as we argue in this chapter, both the Palestinians and Israelis have been hostages to their own histories as well as to each other. In addition, the nature of the contemporary world since 1945 can go some way in explaining the nature of this conflict and the major factors that have dominated it at various junctures.

The themes of the conflict, as we shall discuss in this chapter, embrace many of those tensions that characterize the modern world and its development. Thus it should be made clear that we do not subscribe to the argument that for centuries the Arabs and Jews have been in a fatal atavistic embrace based on primordial hatred. Instead, we agree with Tessler who asserts that, 'both Israel's Jews and Palestinians have legitimate and inalienable rights. These rights are rooted in the historical experience of each people', rather than other factors.[1] Since the early roots of the conflict the battle between Palestinian and Israeli has been about territoriality, identity, ethnicity and religion, economics, competing nationalisms, colonialism and imperialism. Attempts to resolve the conflict, once described as one of the most intractable on earth, have in the past floundered on mutual suspicion and antagonism often exacerbated by the influence of other actors on the conflict. In this chapter we shall discuss these themes rather than present a chronology of events and hostilities.

The Palestinian–Israeli conflict reveals that the divisions that run between Palestinian Arabs and Israeli Jews are multi-faceted. Some might argue that the conflict is a religious and sectarian issue and go some way in agreeing with the primordial argument that there is something inevitable about such a relationship. Others perceive the conflict as ethnic and point to the incompatibility, despite the same semitic origins, of two such distinct groups as Arab and Jew. Some view the deep divisions between Palestinians and Israelis as a result of competing nationalist agendas, each with a unique political view. And still others explain the conflict as a classic class-based colonial paradigm under which only a united working class (Arab and Jewish) will bring about peace and political change. All of these interpretations have had a role to play in explaining why Palestine and its territory became the most enduring battleground of the twentieth century.

For our purposes the examination begins at the end of the nineteenth century. The roots of the conflict lie in ethno-political rather than purely religious differences. Indeed, under the rule of the Ottoman Turks the Jews, Christians and Muslims of Palestine co-existed peacefully. Like all peoples of the region, however, the inhabitants of Palestine were deeply affected by the intervention of the West, not just in terms of ideas and culture but by the consequences of colonial control and foreign penetration of Arab lands. In terms of European ideas and movements, one of the most influential was nationalism. Indeed, the settlement of land by Jews from Europe from the late 1890s onwards was as a direct result of the influence of a new Jewish nationalism entitled Zionism. The congruent origins of the competing nationalisms of Zionism and Palestinian nationalism need to be stressed, not just in the historical context but in terms of explaining the course of the conflict throughout the twentieth century. Indeed it is both remarkable and unfortunate that at the same historical juncture both Jews and Arabs became motivated and conscious of the same themes of self-determination, nationhood and statehood in response to the motifs so strongly associated with nationalism.

'A country without a people for a people without a country'
Chaim Weizman, World Zionist Congress

The emergence of the Jewish nationalism known as Zionism crystallized the desire within the Jewish Diaspora for a Jewish homeland for the Jewish people. Its chief architects, people like Theodor Herzl, a European Jewish intellectual, who in 1896 published a book entitled *The Jewish State*, maintained that assimilation for Jews would never happen and that the Jews should found their own state, preferably in Palestine, the ancient home of the Jewish people. As Gresch and Vidal point out, the link to the former homeland was strong, 'The memory of the lost homeland and the desire to return there were long fostered by religion alone: "Next year in Jerusalem" believers prayed each year'.[2] The call of Zionism was the direct product of hundreds of years of European anti-Semitism and the persecution of Jewish communities, including the Russian pogroms. Zionism was an ideology of its time and place – a product of Western political thought and intellectual trends embracing the nationalist vision.

From 1897, when the first Zionist Congress was convened in Basle in Switzerland, to 1917 the Zionists promoted their vision and lobbied the 'great powers' of USA, Britain, France and Russia for political support. At the same time the first Zionist settlers set off for Palestine to join the pre-existing 50,000 members of the Jewish community there. From 1897 to 1903 some 30,000 Jews emigrated. By 1914 there were 80,000 Jews in Palestine. The Zionist movement in Europe found most sympathy among members of the British government (by this time involved in the First World War), who, through a mixture of hard-headed military strategy and romantic pro-Zionist sentiment, saw some value as part of their war strategy in the Zionist movement. The culmination of this support, as discussed in Chapter 1, was the Balfour Declaration. For the Zionist movement the Declaration, although by no means everything they wanted, was a significant recognition of their cause and their claim to the historic home of the Jewish people in Palestine. In later years, during Britain's mandate of Palestine, however, there were many in the Zionist movement who viewed such patronage with barely disguised frustration and hostility towards their former British friends whom they felt were not wholeheartedly supporting the creation of a Jewish state – not just a Jewish national home.

One major obstacle stood in the way of Zionist aspirations: Palestine's Arab population. Yet, as Gerner points out, for the Zionists 'that Palestine had an existing population . . . was no more relevant than was Kenyan history to the British or Algerian society to the French'.[3] Yet at the same time as Jewish immigration to Palestine increased, new Zionist communities were established, economic methods implemented and society changed, the Palestinians began to organize themselves, establish new nationalist movements and parties in the belief that they had a legitimate right to self-determination alongside others of their Arab brethren across the region. As it was, the Palestinian Arabs could only stand by in dismay as Britain laid claim to their land, as subsequently endorsed by a League of Nations mandate at the end of the First World War. Such decisions, along with continuing tensions with Zionist settlers, further galvanized the Palestinians. The roots of Palestinian nationalism lay in the same rights-based principles as Zionism.

With the establishment throughout the 1920s and early 1930s of nationalist organizations the Palestinian political elite lobbied for change. Neverthe-less, by 1936 such frustrations had reached fever pitch as the Palestinian leadership called a major general strike and the country devolved into a revolt that would last some three years. By 1939 the revolt collapsed in on itself as the Palestinians descended into bitter internecine struggle. In addition the British authorities had deported or imprisoned the major leaders of the Palestinian national movement. In one sense the outcome of this period of the mandate was that the two principal communities of Palestine, in their commitment to competing nationalism, drew an ever-increasing set of boundaries between each other which created economic, religious, cultural and political cleavages that made the likelihood of integration and co-operation increasingly difficult. For example, while the Zionists deliberately pursued a policy of denying employment opportunities to the Arabs, the Arab leadership issued Fatwas against anyone selling land to the Jews. So many increasingly insurmountable frontiers between these communities became a form of partition unanticipated by the country's rulers.

The British struggled for a political solution to the ever-deepening divisions between Jews and Arabs in Palestine under their rule. One commission after another was formed to address the issue. Both the Zionist movement in Palestine and the Palestinian Arab factions were steadily undermining British rule. In 1937 the Peel Commission first proposed the partition of Palestine into an Arab state and a Jewish state, with a third area containing Jerusalem. By 1939 the British announced yet another limit on numbers of Jewish immigrants. This measure would have only a temporary impact and would be turned on its head in the face of the massive tide of Jews fleeing the threat of Hitler's pogroms. By the end of the Second World War the British had thrown in the towel, Clement Atlee had already admitted that Palestine was an 'economic and political liability' and called on the newly formed United Nations to resolve the problem of this 'twice promised land' – which they then attempted to do by opting for partition, as the British had before them. This two-state solution to the conflict between Palestinians and Zionists in Palestine was not acceptable to the Palestinians and triggered further embittered and embattled relations between the two communities for the next half a century.

> On this day that sees the end of the British mandate and in virtue of the natural and historic right of the Jewish people and in accordance with the UN resolution we proclaim the creation of a Jewish state in Palestine.

These were the words with which, on 14 May 1948, David Ben Gurion, leader of the Zionist movement, announced to the world the birth of the state of Israel. He affirmed the new state's claim to legitimacy: that of the Jewish people's right, according to biblical promises made by Jehovah to Abraham.

The new state, however, although recognized by the UN, immediately found itself in confrontation with its Palestinian population and their Arab supporters. Further conflict seemed to be the only item on the agenda. The war of 1948 proved a victory for Israel and a national disaster for the Palestinians, hundreds of thousands of whom found themselves dispossessed of their homes, lands and historic heritage and crammed into squalid refugee camps dispersed across the Arab world. The precise events of the war are widely disputed by historians, and both official Zionist and Arab versions of the events are often misleading. On one side historians such as Karsh assert that 'the Palestinian tragedy was not the inevitable outcome of the Zionist dream but primarily a self-inflicted disaster'.[4] However, 'revisionist' Israeli historians – among them Benny Morris and Ilan Pappe – have started to challenge the official version of events, alleging, among other things, that the newly founded state of Israel was guilty of the deliberate ethnic cleansing of Palestinian communities in the 1948 war.[5]

By the end of the war, the new state of Israel controlled over three-quarters of Palestine, twice as much as originally proposed by the UN. Immigrants settled into many previously Palestinian homes and villages in the new Israeli state. Others were destroyed and deliberately erased from the map. Jerusalem, which the British and UN had declared should be internationalized, became a divided city, the two halves under the respective control of the Israelis and the Jordanians.

There is certainly enough 'evidence' on all sides to generate the important founding myths that are needed to galvanize nations, build new states and sustain liberation movements for many decades. For the Zionists the founding myths of the state and its conflict with the Palestinians have played a part in helping to create a nation from a settler and immigrant community gathered from many parts of the globe. On the other side, the folklore that surrounds the events of the dispossession has played an important part in sustaining a dispossessed and stateless community scattered across the globe. In both cases competing nationalisms and ideological impulses have encouraged many to sustain those myths as important national motifs setting one community apart, once again, from the other.

Those Palestinians finding themselves within the frontier of the new Israeli state became unequal citizens. In more than half a century there has been no sign of integration between the Jews and Arabs of Israel. Separation of these groupings has been officially encouraged; intermarriage is rare and not permitted under religious law in Israel. Schooling, housing and other services are largely confined to one ethnic group or another. This official policy promotes division within Israeli society because it does not embrace the separate but equal philosophy in practice. Arabs and Jews remain unequal parties in many aspects of life.

By May 1948 Israel was established as an independent state and was recognized by the UN. Within the new state, however, a number of ethnic and religious groups vied with each other for power. Palestinian refugees in the Arab world organized themselves politically, embracing and developing a nationalist programme based on the right of self-determination. Their claims and rights were recognized by the UN but were largely ignored in practice by the international community. Within the limitations imposed by the vagaries of Arab authoritarian rule the refugee populations in exile planned their liberation.

From this point it appeared that intractable lines of conflict were drawn between the Israelis and the Palestinians. Political solutions to conflict were in short supply and focused on the tried and largely unsuccessful formula of partition that, given its ineffectiveness in promoting the resolution of other ethnic disputes, namely Ireland, was questionable in the first place. Throughout the 1950s and 1960s, as Israel embarked on a major process of state consolidation, there emerged sharp divisions over the proposed frontier of the state. On the right-wing, the Zionist goal of establishing a Jewish state in the whole of Eretz Israel (biblical Israel) was developed and publicly debated. Such expansionist plans held potentially dangerous threats. These aspirations, though not shared by all political leaders, only condemned Israel and the Palestinians to further conflict. The majority of Israelis clung tenaciously to their new state, enshrined its Jewish identity through the law of the 'Right of Return', founded in the aftermath of the Holocaust, and dedicated themselves to safeguarding themselves and future generations. The maintenance of the security of the state and its people, surrounded as they were by so many neighbours who were enemies, became a major preoccupation of the political establishment, with the military gobbling up a consistently large share of the country's gross domestic product. Israeli leaders claimed that they were not courting further conflict but rather seeking to establish the security of the state for present and future generations.

If, as we noted in Chapter 1, the Israeli victory of 1967 meant that Israel got more than it bargained for in terms of the newly acquired territories and the Palestinian Arab populations of the West Bank, Arab East Jerusalem (including the old city) and the Gaza Strip, there was also evidence of splits within the political establishment over what strategy to adopt next. While it is true that the Israelis have remained in continuous occupation of these lands ever since, there have always been opposing arguments for the maintenance of Israeli control (or sovereignty) of such territories. From a strategic point of view, by holding on to the West Bank, for example, Israel could better defend its borders and major centres of population. On the other hand, there were some who believed that if land were traded for peace with its Arab neighbours, then relinquishing the West Bank or elsewhere would be worth it. By and large, however, the strategic arguments have prevailed and remain an important aspect of the present-day peace negotiations between Israel and the Palestinians.

While the Israeli occupation has been a military one, the strategic foothold established in the West Bank, the Gaza Strip and the Golan Heights has been facilitated by the settlement of Israeli Jews on large parts of Palestinian land in direct contravention of UN resolutions on the issue. Many types of settlement activity, some ideologically motivated, others religiously and yet more 'paramilitary security' based, emerged over the ensuing decades and were tacitly supported by the state. The settlement of Palestinian land started in earnest in the early 1970s and by the late 1990s hundreds of thousands of Israeli Jews were living in such illegally constructed settlements in the West Bank and Gaza Strip, and were proving to be a major and growing obstacle to the resolution of the Palestinian–Israeli conflict. Even American threats in the 1990s to halt soft loans to Israel failed to stop the support offered by successive Israeli governments to the right-wing-led settler movement, many of whom were financed by members of the Jewish Zionist Diaspora especially in the United States.[6] Settlement activity has created new demographic realities that Israel is committed to. Nevertheless, the future of the settlements remains a key item on the agenda for the final status negotiations.

Since 1967 the Palestinians, through the extension of their commitment to nationalism, have established formidable political movements for national liberation and self-determination. The best known of these groups is the Palestine Liberation Organization (PLO), officially established in 1964, an umbrella organization representing four major nationalist factions: Fatah, the Communists, the Democratic Front for the Liberation of Palestine (DFLP) and the Popular Front for the Liberation of Palestine (PFLP). In 1968 the PLO fell under the control of Yasser Arafat and his comrades. Although the organization is large, bureaucratic and extremely factional, it has attempted to provide for and serve the Palestinian refugee community, conducted an armed struggle, and represents to the rest of the world the legitimate rights of the Palestinian people to self-determination and independence. Regarded as the 'legitimate' representative of the Palestinian people, including the refugee population, this movement, and its often dissident offshoots, has engaged in a struggle for national liberation. Over its forty-odd years engaged in 'armed struggle', the PLO and other Palestinian dissidents have been involved in acts of political violence such as hijackings, bomb attacks and assassinations against Israel and its representatives abroad, including American Jews. It has confronted two major Arab states – Jordan in 1970 and Lebanon between 1975 and 1982 where it became engaged in civil conflict with state authorities and was accused of running a 'state within a state' for major Palestinian refugee communities resident in both countries.[7] Indeed, until the late 1980s the Palestinians were regarded as synonymous with terrorism the world over. Supporters of Palestinian rights to self-determination argued that this strategy to engage in terrorism was part of a cycle of desperation at a time when they were denied political rights or statehood. Many others, however, particularly in policy-making circles in Tel Aviv, Washington and other Western capitals, were not prepared to tolerate the pursuit of politics through the barrel of a gun.

Eventually the Palestinian nationalist call to arms was set aside in 1988 when PLO leader Yasser Arafat literally delivered an olive branch at a specially convened meeting of the UN general assembly in Geneva. At this event Arafat declared, 'we totally and absolutely renounce all forms of terrorism, including individual, group and state terrorism'.[8] The statement was considered a clear indication that the PLO sought full admission into the international fold. It would take five more years before the announcement of Israel's decision to recognize the PLO as legitimate representatives of the Palestinians and the initiation of the peace process that in 1993 culminated in an agreement for limited Palestinian autonomy and an agenda for final status negotiations between the two sides. Until that time in early 1993 the Palestinians and Israelis appeared to live in two separate worlds, each denying the right of existence to the other. The path to resolving the conflict would be a long and tough one.

The two communities, however separate in terms of political co-existence, have not lived in total isolation from each other. Hostility and mutual antagonism, however, often characterize relations. Within Israeli society the state functions very much like any other liberal democracy, where regular and free elections are held, the citizens are enfranchised and the electoral system is one of proportional representation based on a single constituency. Yet, in the occupied territories the Israeli state, obsessed with security, has often acted in an authoritarian and repressive fashion. Until 1993 the Palestinian population was governed by a myriad of military orders requiring permits for every aspect of their lives and eschewing any attempt by the Palestinian community to take power for itself and determine its own affairs. Israelis, on the other hand, believed they lived under the constant threat of Palestinian attacks from all quarters. Such fears were compounded by the very real threats posed by an organization dedicated to armed struggle in the realization of its goals. While hundreds of thousands of Palestinians worked in Israel as day labourers, they were compelled by Israeli law to return to their homes over the Green Line by nightfall. While some friendships did grow, they were largely an exception to a rule on both sides that kept the two communities apart. Although economically tied together, there were very few political, religious or cultural motifs that were common or shared between the two communities. Even in Jerusalem, Israel's so-called 'united capital', Israelis and Palestinians lived very different lives from each other and few urban spaces were available for all to feel a part of.

In addition it has to be noted that the economic relationship between Israel and the Palestinians has been directly exploitative on Israel's part. The occupied territories became Israel's largest export market and source of cheap labour, and the Palestinian economy was crippled and penalized in return.[9] Until the outbreak of the Palestinian uprising, or Intifada, in 1987 there was also evidence of growing support on the Israeli right for the annexation of the West Bank. Annexation would provide a direct economic benefit to Israel. There was only one problem facing the annexationist lobby and this was the issue of what to do with the Palestinian population of the area. By this point a number of political groupings and parties had emerged advocating 'transfer' or the 'mass deportation' of Palestinians to Arab states like Jordan. Indeed, in 1987 the mainstream Israeli press were willing to air debates entitled 'Jordan is Palestine' that openly promoted 'transfer' as a solution to the growing demographic threat within the occupied West Bank.

Within the Palestinian community there was growing resentment and frustration at the restrictions they faced in everyday life. Any form of political activity was criminalized by the military authorities. The PLO was outlawed, people were banned from free assembly, public meetings were forbidden. Membership of political organizations was punishable by long prison sentences, often without trial. By the late 1980s, with the PLO expelled from Lebanon, Jewish settlement continuing apace and the 'iron fist' of occupation in almost perpetual stranglehold, a sense of desperation began to permeate Palestinian ranks. In the West Bank and Gaza the Palestinian refugees felt increasingly abandoned by their Arab brethren who appeared preoccupied with other regional matters. The international community held little sympathy for Palestinian 'terrorists' and Israel, bolstered by a 'special relationship' with the USA, despite its illegal acts of settlement in the West Bank and Gaza Strip, seemed untouchable.

The outbreak of the uprising (Intifada) in December 1987 marked the culmination of growing political awareness among young Palestinians and starkly exposed the fault line in this conflict between Palestinian and Israeli. The long-term goals of the uprising were articulated as a desire to bring an end to the Israeli occupation of the West Bank and Gaza Strip and the establishment of a Palestinian state. In the short term the plan was to disengage from the structure of the Israeli occupation as much as possible and achieve a greater level of Palestinian self-reliance and unity of purpose. The local economy, for example, was boosted through consumers boycotting Israeli products.

The Intifada was a major turning point in the Palestinian–Israeli conflict. The Palestinians, through the quickly established framework of the Intifada, indicated that they were rejecting anything that represented Israeli rule over their lives. The Palestinians were sending a message that said 'No' to Israeli control. This mass rebellion also communicated an important message to the PLO leadership in Tunis, and as Khalidi asserts 'betokened a realisation by the PLO leadership that the future of the movement lay in Palestine, rather than outside it'.[10] It is widely acknowledged that this popular-based uprising took the PLO and other Palestinian leaders by surprise as much as Israel.

But the question we must now ask is: did the Intifada galvanize the Israelis and Palestinians into seeking a solution to the deep breach between them? The Intifada shook Israel because of its spontaneous and widespread nature. This was portrayed positively in the international media which flocked to Israel and the occupied territories to film poignant scenes such as small boys having their bones deliberately broken by Israeli soldiers acting under the express orders of Defence Minister Yitzhak Rabin. Initially the Intifada was not a planned event but rather a very powerful and spontaneous Palestinian protest against the everyday indignities inflicted by Israeli control. The first months of the uprising were characterized by mass demonstrations involving every sector of society. The international media's portrayal of women and children, the young and the old demonstrating with such passion went some considerable way in rehabilitating or altering the perception of Palestinians, not as terrorists but as victims of a military occupation that had lasted some twenty years.

The widely supported spontaneous nature of the uprising was quickly harnessed by locally based committees, which were formed to help people at every level. The establishment of the United National Leadership of the Uprising (UNLU) – representing all factions of the PLO and the Islamic movements Hamas and Islamic Jihad – to harness and provide direction to the uprising also represented a major development in Palestinian politics. It demonstrated the maturity of the local political leadership when pursuing a national agenda. The Israelis had no immediately successful answer to the campaign of mass civil disobedience. Their army, trained and prepared for combat on the battlefield, was often faced with an enemy made up of unarmed women, children and young people whose major weapon against Israel's hi-tech armoury was rocks and Molotovs. The Palestinians had from the outset decided to refrain from the use of firearms against the Israeli army and settlers – a highly successful ploy, which played well internationally.

However, as the first, second and third anniversaries of the uprising were commemorated a number of disturbing factors were becoming apparent. First, the uprising was only serving to deepen divisions between Israelis and Palestinians. However objectionable the policies of the occupation, it had at least forced some level of daily contact between the Israelis and Palestinians. The uprising ruptured this tentative relationship that had built up over twenty years. Each group retreated into the laager of their own society, cross-community contacts were frowned upon and treated with mistrust as dangerously disloyal.

Second, this atmosphere of war-like, low-intensity combat meant that informal channels for conflict resolution were eroded or eliminated. As the first attacks on Israelis were undertaken by Palestinian groups, particularly the Islamic forces of Hamas and Islamic Jihad, groups in Israeli society like Peace Now were ridiculed and marginalized. Accordingly the Israeli right gained increased support because of their resolutely anti-Palestinian stance. Indeed, in the 1988 Israeli election, the Israeli right succeeded in winning a victory at the polls and heading the National Unity government. Moreover, extremism and religious radicalism found support within the respective communities in both Israel and Palestine.

Third, the uprising challenged overnight the status quo in the occupied territories. Attempts to quell the uprising by the Israeli army proved ineffective, which in turn affected army morale and led to public debate in Israel about the role of the army. The Israelis were faced with a stark fact; that they had to do something about the Palestinian issue and had to accept that previous talk of annexation or even maintaining the status quo ante was now completely out of the question. In addition international pressure was making itself felt to an unprecedented extent within the Israeli political establishment. The international mass media had transmitted film for prime time viewing of Israel's soldiers taking on unarmed women and children. Commentators criticized Israel's treatment of the Palestinians, and human rights abuses were publicly pilloried. Both at home and abroad many Jews began to question, for the first time, the efficacy of the occupation of the West Bank and Gaza Strip. This exposed fissures and tensions from within the Jewish community, undermining the previous solidarity of public opinion. For once the Arabs were ahead in the PR battle for international opinion.

It was also clear that the fissure between the Palestinians and the Israelis had become so deep rooted that the only solution was to offer some glimmer of a negotiated peace process. As it happened, however, it was one other event, well away from the West Bank and Gaza Strip, that was to create the conditions for decisive change, encouraging all the parties involved, including most importantly the Americans, to make a concerted effort to kick-start the peace process.

The Iraqi invasion of Kuwait on 2 August 1990 and the ensuing Gulf crisis (see Chapter 8) had important implications for the Palestinian–Israeli conflict. Most importantly it stimulated an American-led initiative to secure some kind of Arab–Israeli peace process in the Middle East. In the wake of the crisis the US sought to re-establish stability in the region, and once again recognized that at the heart of any settlement between Israel and the Arab states was the Palestinian issue. This had to be addressed. With the eclipse of the Soviet Union and the emergence of a 'new world order' a historic opportunity to go for peace was now at hand. The moment also provided the Americans, the remaining superpower, with a chance to dictate the peace they envisioned rather than rely on one promoted by actual parties to the conflict.

The right-wing Likud government in Israel, led by the then Prime Minister Yitzhak Shamir, refused, however, to enter into any direct discussion with the Palestinian leadership. His government still refused to recognize the PLO and made it clear that the most that Palestinians could ever hope to achieve under his government was a limited form of autonomy (similar to those discussed with Sadat at Camp David) in which Israel would retain ultimate control over the West Bank and Gaza Strip. It was under these unpromising preconditions, with the Jordanians providing a cover for the Palestinian negotiators, that the historic first round of Arab–Israeli peace talks were convened under the auspices of the USA and the former USSR in November 1991 in Madrid. Thus a spontaneous mass rebellion in coincidental conjunction with a war elsewhere in the region temporarily and unprecedentedly united East and West. For a variety of reasons, which in one way or another had a linkage back to the dynamics of the Israeli–Palestinian conflict, this proved to be the catalyst in promoting a new attempt at a negotiated settlement of the conflict between the Palestinians and Israel.

Within Israel the election of a Labour government in June 1992 on a pro-peace platform reflected Intifada fatigue within the electorate. This was recognized both at home and abroad as a brave step within the larger national framework of debate about security versus peace. The Intifada had directly affected many sectors of Israeli society – through the increased deployment of Israeli conscript and reserve troops to the West Bank and Gaza Strip and the issue of Palestinian labour in Israel. Ordinary Israelis no longer felt free to travel without fear in the West Bank and Gaza Strip, and increasingly by the early 1990s a new form of fatal attack was taken over the 1967 border into Israeli cities like Tel Aviv in the form of car and suicide bomb attacks carried out by Hamas and Islamic Jihad. In this new political climate secret negotiations were subsequently proposed and approved in left-leaning Israeli circles and met with the cautious approval of Prime Minister Rabin himself. In public the formal Madrid process floundered as one obstacle to negotiation after another stymied the ineffectual attempts on all sides to get to grips with the main issues.

As we now know, while the official peace process was seen to stagnate throughout 1993, Israel and the PLO had opened a highly secret channel of negotiations in Norway. These culminated – to universal surprise – in the official White House ceremony and signing of the Declaration of Principles (DoP). The DoP, or Oslo Accords as they are now referred to, permitted limited and phased autonomy in the West Bank and Gaza Strip. They also provided a future framework for the peaceful resolution of the most important issues pertaining to the Israeli–Palestinian conflict: land, Jerusalem, refugees, settlements, security and borders. This was the event that produced the stage-managed handshake between Rabin and Arafat with which we started this chapter. Stage-management, however, would not be enough to establish a meaningful process of trust-building between Israel and the Palestinians and the conclusion of final status peace talks outlined under the Oslo framework. The peace process was stymied and bedevilled at almost every turn. The reality and pressures of transition and peace-building shattered dreams on both sides of the divide. In Israel Yitzhak Rabin was assassinated, the right-wing Likud gained new ascendency on an anti-negotiation platform, troops were not ordered to deploy according to agreed timetables. Life under the newly established Palestinian Authority, led by PLO-leader Yasser Arafat, failed to deliver security, economic or political dividends for the Palestinians. Islamist violence against Israel, manifest in suicide bombs over the 1948 border, added new dimensions to the conflict and attempts to establish security and peace at one and the same time. The election of a Labour government led by former army general Ehud Barak on a pro-peace platform in 1999 promoted an illusion that peace might become possible again. Yet the bitter fall-out and absence of genuine compromise on final status issues dogged the talks process throughout 1999 and 2000. Palestinian frustration at perceived Israeli arrogance crystallized around the deliberately provocative visit of former Likud Minister Ariel Sharon to Jerusalem's Islamic holy site the Dome of the Rock in September 2000 and a new Intifada broke out. Since that time death and violence has superseded peace and reconciliation, and the shallow foundations of the Oslo Peace have been exposed. Both sides believe, once again, that they are engaged in a war of independence in which there can only be one victor and the enemy must be vanquished. Peace through negotiation fell into abeyance and in the absence of sustained American pressure the two sides to conflict have fallen back into deep suspicion of each other.

Now that a 'road map' sponsored by the quartet (UN, US, Russia and the EU) has been formally tabled as a kick-start to a new MEPP, mutual suspicions need to be banished and both sides will have to negotiate with flexibility and good faith. How easy that sounds! How often have we been here before since Oslo! The 'road map' is particularly difficult for the hard men of the PA and of the State of Israel. American pressure will be needed to deliver the hard right government of Ariel Sharon. This presents a major challenge to George W. Bush. Not only will he have to overcome strong Israeli obduracy but also win over his own hard men of the American right, many of whom identify with the Israelis as strategic partners in the global war against terror. Forthcoming elections in the US, with the Zionist lobby in full cry in the defence of any perceived threat to Israel, will not make his task easier. As for the PA, the new Prime Minister also has an uphill task selling the 'road map' to his people. It is perceived by many as being loaded against the Palestinians with the onus on the Arab side to stop hostilities before the Israelis are called upon to do anything. And the very fact that Abu Ma'azen is seen as an acceptable partner in negotiations by the Israeli government (unlike President Yasir Arafat, categorized by Sharon as the Palestinian Bin Laden) is a hard blow to the credibility of the new Prime Minister. He is for that reason regarded by many Palestinian radicals as too flexible (and too pro-Western) to be an effective and tough leader facing the old enemy at a crucial time. Omens therefore remain inauspicious.

3   Superpower conflict in the Middle East

War by proxy

The rivalry between the United States and the former Soviet Union has made a major contribution to the dynamics of politics and conflicts in the Middle East. From the end of the Second World War to the present day the influence of American interests and, until 1990, Soviet interests and ambitions in the Middle East was easily discernible. The turning point in this superpower competition was the Gulf crisis in 1990 when an economically debilitated and politically weakened Soviet Union bowed out of the race with the United States and Soviet President Gorbachev gave US President George Bush his backing in the Allies' effort to end the Iraqi occupation of Kuwait. Until that point both had competed for influence in the region in an attempt to safeguard oil interests and strategic routes. Throughout this period neither side was willing to let the other steal an ideological march in a part of the world that was regarded as so vital to both superpowers and, in particular, the oil-dependent industrialized nations of the West.

The Middle East was an extension of the cold war theatre between the USSR and the USA for four decades. The impact of the cold war in contributing both to the rise in tension and the growth of conflict made its mark in the area, particularly throughout the 1950s, 1960s and 1970s. In seeking to extend their influence over the region, both the United States and the Soviet Union engaged in attempts to create 'client' states that would act as local proxies and allies. In pursuing this strategy policy-makers in Moscow and Washington exploited new fissures and tensions, severely exacerbating pre-existing ones such as the Arab–Israeli conflict.

This extension of superpower rivalry to the Middle East did not occur overnight. The growth of Soviet and American power and influence gradually filled a vacuum created by the post-war decline of former colonial powers, notably Britain and France. Keen to step into the breach, the USA in particular made an early start and tried to remain a step ahead of the Russians in its attempt to protect strategic interests in the region. In the wake of the Second World War newly exploited oil and pressure from American commercial interests were the major motives for Washington's involvement in the area. But, as Chomsky noted, 'At the rhetorical level, the threat from which the Middle East must be "defended" is generally pictured to be the USSR.'[1] Thus, from the first days of the Truman Doctrine in 1947 to the turbulent months of 1990 when the US led the Allied forces into conflict in the 'Mother of all Battles' with Iraq, the impact of the superpowers on regional issues was immense.

The outcome of the superpower conflict, as this chapter will illustrate, was a confrontation from which the USA, despite its emergence as the dominant power in a 'new world order', failed to emerge as a clear victor. The arena in which the two sides engaged in a battle of proxies is littered with the legacy of major arms races, client–patron relationships and uneasy alliances that run counter to the national interest of many of the states in the region. While it is true that there were many other 'battlefields' in the cold war, the Middle East, due to its oil and its strategic position, seems to have suffered most.

According to Rodinson, in its attempts to limit Soviet influence, the American 'effort to enrol the Arabs in the coalition encircling the Communist world had in fact driven the Arab peoples, profoundly uninterested in the struggle for world mastery, into a sympathetic attitude towards the hated power'.[2] This was a cold war in which, when the Berlin Wall came down in 1989, pundits and policy-makers alike found there was little of value to commemorate in the posturing and ideological battles that had been waged in the previous decades. In their post-cold war questioning they increasingly doubted whether the former Soviet Union had posed the 'real' threat they had widely believed it had.

In March 1947, as Europe embarked on the reconstruction of nations rent asunder by war, US President Harry Truman announced a new doctrine for the Middle East that would have a major impact on emerging conflicts and future tensions in decades to come. Fearful of a Soviet expansion of power through Eastern Europe and onto the shores of the Mediterranean and the Arab world, the US government announced its intention of containing the Soviet threat. Each administration from Truman onwards reiterated similar commitments to resist the spread of Soviet influence, thereby safe-guarding the Western world's access to oil and other strategic interests. Yet one factor, which was to complicate Washington's attempt to influence the Arab and Muslim states, was America's 'special relationship' with Israel. In fact this relationship was initially slow to develop. Intensive support for Israel did not become a major policy plank of the US until the late 1950s. Up to the Suez crisis, for example, France was the major arms supplier (and military partner) of Israel.

Thus, as Lesch has pointed out, while the 'value of the Middle East became contemporaneously linked to the emerging cold war between the United States and the Soviet Union', the special link with the state of Israel 'also complicated Washington's relations with and objectives towards the Arab world as Arabs increasingly perceived US and Israeli interests as being one and the same'.[3] Over the decades the legislators in the American Congress have remained largely sympathetic to Israel, voting through bills extending massive financial and military support. The pro-Israel lobby in the United States may have had to weather some significant spats with successive political administrations yet it has still been recognized as a significant pressure on the American government, policy-makers and opinion-formers across the country. While it is easy to be wary about the sincerity of statements such as the one made by former President Jimmy Carter that 'It's absolutely crucial that no one in our country or around the world ever doubt that our number one commitment in the Middle East is to protect the right of Israel to exist', it is only the depth of sincerity that is questioned when held up against the whole gamut of American national interests.[4] What Carter and other US presidents were really saying was that, given the powerful influence of the Zionist (pro-Israel) lobby in US domestic politics, it would be a bold or rash administration that took any action that might arouse its ire. Especially at election time! And so experience has proved.

There are a number of objectives that the US has consistently pursued over the years in determining their policies towards the Middle East and bilateral relations with the Arab and other states of that region. These broad objectives are as follows:

Economic and commercial: to maintain the steady flow of Iranian and Arab oil to the Western states of the capitalist world. Arab oil was, and remains, vital to Western interests; without it GNP in the US would be cut by 13 per cent. In addition an objective within this sphere is to promote the interests of US companies throughout the region, especially in the wealthy markets of the Gulf states including Saudi Arabia.

Containment: to prevent perceived Soviet expansionism. The United States saw it as its objective (especially following the Soviet invasion of Afghanistan in 1979 and the collapse of the pro-American regime in Iran) to 'protect' the independence of the Arab states and to defend their free choice to continue to supply oil to the West unhindered by the Soviet Union or any of its allies in the area.

Commitment: to maintain not only the security but also the prosperity of Israel. This is the essence of the 'special relationship'. The United States perceived Israel as a strategic ally and their regional partner. The drawback is that this policy has threatened and continues to undermine Arab–American relations and endangers US commercial interests in the wider region.

Aid: to use aid as a strategic tool. As an instrument of American foreign policy aid has secured the dependency and often grudging fealty of the region's largest state, Egypt, and by the mid-1990s had succeeded in bringing Jordan firmly into the aid-dependent American orbit. In addition Israel has traditionally enjoyed a privileged position in the receipt of US government subsidy, receiving more per capita assistance than any other country in the world. In 1997 alone Israel had received some $240 million of non-military assistance from the US.

Arms: to maintain the arms balance in the Middle East. The United States has been involved in supplying a number of states with weaponry. In so doing it has sought to ensure that the balance tips in the favour of its clients, thus brokering a multi-billion dollar industry that has armed and even trained such disparate clients as the pre-revolutionary Iran, Afghan anti-Soviet guerrillas, the Israelis and the Saudis. Israel, for example, has received billions of dollars in arms in grants from the US. In addition, between 1982 and 1986 Egypt was in receipt of a $2.4 billion grant from the US government for the purchase of American arms and military supplies.[5]

These objectives, which underpin American policy in the Middle East, also determine its basic features. The first feature is the desire by the US to disadvantage Western competitors. Under cover of the 'open door' policy, the US has assured itself an indisputable supremacy both in political influence and commercial matters – as Chomsky has observed in the case of Iran in 1953 where 'one consequence of the CIA-backed coup that restored the Shah . . . was to transfer 40 per cent of Iranian oil from British to American hands'.[6] This policy was pursued with growing success: first after the Second World War with the promulgation of the Truman Doctrine, then following Suez with the Eisenhower Doctrine. By the 1970s, with the waning of British influence in the Gulf, the US stepped into the breach and more recently in the same area it has extracted commercial contracts as a quid pro quo for its support for the Gulf monarchies in the aftermath of the Kuwait crisis. The same policy is already being followed in 'liberated' Iraq where the downfall of the regime in April 2003 was immediately followed by the American-controlled interim administration by granting contracts for reconstruction projects exclusively to US companies.

The second feature was the attempt to form a massive regional alliance directed against the Soviet Union and its local allies. This attempt at alliance-making quickly paid dividends in the north (Greece, Turkey, monarchist

Iran), but failed in the south where any prospect of co-operation between Israel and the Arab countries inevitably ran up against the obstacle of the Palestinian issue.

The third and final feature was the determination to resort to any means, including military, to pursue these aims – as illustrated in Lebanon in 1958 and during the Gulf crisis of 1990 to 1991. As Alin argues, the motives for America's involvement in the civil crisis in Lebanon in 1958 were clear, 'By sending US troops to Lebanon, the Eisenhower administration sought to uphold Western interests in the Middle East against the perceived challenge of Arab nationalism and to a lesser extent, communism.'[7] There were also sound commercial reasons. Lebanon was a valuable market for American business, especially as a banking centre, and it was important for would-be US investors that stability be restored.[8]

At various stages of US involvement in the region policy has been affected to a greater or lesser degree by these objectives, and some have assumed more importance than others at different times. Nevertheless, successive US administrations have expressed a clear commitment to achieve these goals in furtherance of the American national interest. Sometimes the convenient ideological cloak of democracy, freedom and the virtues of capitalism has been used in support of apparently contradictory military and other actions but few have ever been truly convinced that US interest in the region stems purely from the ideological pledge to promote and protect democracy. Indeed, American policy-makers have often been prepared to prop up and assist authoritarian and anti-democratic regimes in the Middle East if such actions furthered the protection of US strategic and commercial interests. Support for Saddam's Iraq against Khomeini's Iran is a case in point, as is the US relationship with Saudi Arabia. The role of the CIA in training the anti-Soviet Afghan Mujahideen in the 1980s is another example.

Following US diplomatic intervention in the Suez crisis (against Britain and France) and the brief interlude in Lebanon in 1958, a reorientation of American activity in terms of implementation became apparent. During the 1960s and early 1970s US policy in the region was restructured. As Soviet influence and Arab nationalist hostility grew, Washington's reluctance to supply advanced weaponry abated. The war of 1967 transformed the military and political balance in the region, and Israel's relationship with the US became strengthened as Washington increasingly affirmed the Jewish state as a reliable partner. Soviet influence over Syria and Egypt in the wake of the war and the intensification of ideological and other forms of support to the Palestinian guerrilla movement on the other side was also increasingly apparent. This policy was pursued throughout the Nixon administration and the furtherance of this relationship was seen in terms of an economic-military strategy.

American policy shifted again after the 1973 Arab–Israeli war and the use of oil as a weapon by the Arab states to support Egypt and Syria. There was a discernible policy shift towards recognizing the significance for US interests of the conservative Arab regimes, although Israel and Iran were still supported by the increasingly influential pro-Israel lobby in America. Hoping to win friends and influence the right people, American foreign policy-makers used arms sales, for example, as the lever in bolstering US–Saudi relations. In overcoming opposition, both at home and abroad, to the policy of encouraging a closer relationship with the Gulf monarchies, the US used the sale of arms as a general panacea. Such a strategy not only boosted the American arms industry but accelerated both the arms race between Arab and other states and also the competition against the Soviet Union, who also played the 'arms' card on a regular basis with its regional clients.

In 1979 the Iranian revolution was a severe setback for US ambitions and its influence in the area. The fall of the pro-American Shah left the area of the Gulf without an influential reliable client for the United States. Israel remained the only credible ally in the Middle East with no worthwhile backup from either the Iranians or Arabs. Indeed, the new regime in Iran was bitterly anti-American, characterizing Washington as the 'Big Satan'. Aware of the undue influence this might give Israel and the lack of a reliable and influential ally in the Arab camp, US policy-makers, according to Stork *et al.*, 'were suddenly desperate for a short-term resolution to Arab–Israeli differences in a manner that could embrace Egypt as a sort of strategic apprentice and avoid debilitating tensions with Israel'.[9] In addition the revolutionary leadership in Tehran capitalized on American vulnerability in the area to engage the US on another ideological battlefront, this time between the forces of Islamism and imperialist satanic America.

In an attempt to contain Soviet ambitions in Afghanistan, on the doorstep of both Iran and Pakistan, and seeking to block Ayatollah Khomeini's efforts to 'export' Islamic revolution, successive US administrations led by Presidents Carter and Reagan became increasingly embroiled in the major conflicts in the region, including support for the Mujahideen in Afghanistan, and assistance to Saddam Hussein's Iraq during its war with Iran throughout the 1980s. American troops were also sent to Lebanon again in an abortive attempt to restore stability, and there was also the Irangate scandal (see Chapter 7). There was barely a major or minor encounter in the region that in some way was not either openly or covertly influenced by US machinations or involvement.

Indeed, the 1980s were marked by an increasingly apparent tension between US intentions and strategic goals vis-à-vis the region and local resistance to such objectives. Old relationships were put under strain, such as that between Israel and the United States, when Israel sought to pursue its own interests even at the expense of its patrons in Washington. Efforts by US administrators in 1982 to revitalize the Arab–Israeli peace process through the Reagan Plan were an ill-disguised attempt to appease Israel and bring it back under American direction.[10] The fact that some forty years since the end of war, and the falling of the Iron Curtain dividing Europe, the superpower conflict and the perceived Soviet threat was still a major feature of US interest in the Middle East was remarkable. Nevertheless, the Reagan administration and that of his successor George Bush did achieve some small successes for US policy. The PLO was largely neutralized; Egypt was firmly held within the American camp. Iraq was used to prevent Iran (for the large part) from threatening oil interests in the Gulf area and shipping lanes were kept open. The Mujahideen in Afghanistan, trained and armed by the CIA, successfully battled against the Soviet army and its local proxies, and Iran and other pro-Soviet states such as Syria were successfully characterized as international pariahs and quarantined accordingly.

The conflict against the Soviet Union, which over more than forty years had brought other disputes and tensions into its orbit and absorbed them, looked set to continue for another fifty years and well into the new millennium until those fateful days in the early 1990s when the Communist regimes in the Soviet Union and the states of Eastern Europe unravelled. From that point on, the former Soviet Union – consisting as its now does of many states from Russia, Estonia and Latvia to Kazakhstan, Armenia and Azerbaijan – would not possess the influence and strength to challenge American hegemony in the Middle East. But the previous four decades told a different story.

Quite simply the history of the Soviet Union and its role in the Middle East can be addressed by looking at one question: Was Soviet policy designed to support the world-wide advance of communism and socialism or was it more definitely cast to support its own national security interests? Studying this question in the context of some forty-odd years throws up some conflicting evidence.

During the 1940s Moscow tried to take advantage of post-war confusion in order to build up its influence and create new zones of influence on its south-western as well as Eastern European borders. Although the Soviets emphasized ideological objectives, their commitment to aid was small due to their own war-ravaged economy. The way chosen therefore (in accordance with the 'spread revolution' concept) was to support leftist opposition groups without too much concern for relations with individual governments.

In the 1950s, under Khrushchev, policy changed; this period has come to be described as the 'courtship phase'. Under the threat of encirclement from the West through the Baghdad Pact, which was essentially an anti-Soviet alliance in the region spearheaded by the USA, the USSR again gained access to the Middle Eastern theatre. It accepted non-alignment as a potentially positive attitude, even supported it, perceiving it as essentially 'anti-Western', and exploited the benefits of that policy through the Czech arms deal with Egypt in 1955. However, its involvement in the region still remained limited and cordial relations with Arab states were largely a result of anti-Western feeling rather than pro-Soviet sentiments.

Only in the 1960s does hard evidence of Soviet attempts to consolidate its political role in the Middle East emerge. In 1963, for example, it requested a base in Egypt. The US continued to be perceived as a threat, hence the Soviet Union's renewed emphasis on military expansion and consolidation in the area, embodied in the establishment of the Mediterranean Squadron. Consolidation of power and the establishment of a condominium with the US based on a relationship of parity became the main aims of Soviet policy.

Following the wars of 1967 and 1973 the two superpowers realized the wisdom and necessity of détente, having very nearly come into direct nuclear confrontation via their local protégés during the 1973 hostilities. Yet the Soviet Union was still willing to maintain its influence with its allies – taking Egypt's side during the conflict in Yemen. During this period the Soviets enjoyed a fairly strong relationship with the 'progressive' or 'radical' Arab states (Egypt, Syria, Iraq), but it was already clear that they were mainly reacting to developments that they did not really control – this was no proactive embrace of revolutionary socialism nor were the ideologues in the Kremlin so idealistic as to believe that pragmatism did not have its role to play in these relationships. Thus, for every copy of the *Communist Manifesto* shipped from Moscow to the Arab capitals, there were many other more practical 'gifts': boxes of ammunition, shipments of tanks, MiG warplanes and scholarships for doctors and engineers. Other forms of practical assistance were also forthcoming as indications of Soviet support, although many items, especially military hardware, were not free nor were they always representative of the cutting edge of Soviet technology.

From 1973 Soviet influence in the region began to wane. Even such friendly regimes as Syria and Iraq did very much as they liked when their aims were criticized for conflicting with those of the USSR. On the whole the USSR had little real influence in the Middle East, and no success in actually bringing about changes in leadership. They even had very little hold over the local Arab Communist parties: the regional backlash against the Communist plot in Sudan in 1971, which the Soviets had advised against, probably meant the beginning of the end for Soviet ideological appeal in the area as a whole. Any improvement of Soviet standing that did occur was really only success by default, caused by playing one superpower off against the other.

In any case it was clear that Soviet policy in the Middle East had under-gone a shift – particularly since the 1960s when, as McLaurin notes, 'a noticeable status quo element made itself felt in Soviet foreign policy'; and this was indeed reflected in the conduct of Soviet policy in the Middle East.[11] Some non-Communist regimes were supported, the Arab–Israeli conflict was 'managed' carefully and restraint was shown in arms sales to local allies (qualitatively rather than quantitatively). All this seems to confirm the view that détente and state interests were, at least since the 1960s, all-important for the USSR. Ideology and support for the 'progressive' tendencies were of minor concern and were often used to justify the means in selling such policies to a domestic Soviet audience. However, this view does not give the full picture.

The Soviets perceived their own aims in a different light. Dawisha and Dawisha note that there was a clear strategy based on the concept of the 'correlation of forces', which is 'as much a definition of power as it is a formula for the application of power based on the notion of not maintaining the status quo but transforming it'.[12] There were four elements to this policy:

1   Manipulation of class consciousness.
2   Short-term aims should further long-term goals.
3   Regional policy must be determined with reference to global strategy.
4   The wider interests of Soviet socialism should always take priority over the parochial interests of national liberation movements. Accordingly, the maintenance of the security of the borders of the Soviet Union must take precedence over national liberation movements.

This in itself forms a basic principle of Soviet strategy. In addition, one difficulty in pursuing such a policy related to the dissonance between Soviet objectives and local factors, which effectively acted as a constraint on Soviet ambition.

Most of the Soviet Union's policies can be explained with reference to the above framework, which appears to be designed to avoid risk of conflict, particularly through confrontation with the USA. Soviet attitudes towards support for 'progressive regimes' remained desirable since they opposed imperialism; however, the USSR's strategic interests were more important and in certain circumstances led to withdrawal of such support. Even support for individual parties could be abandoned in favour of bourgeois national liberation movements if this became necessary for wider strategic reasons. These conclusions run counter to McLaurin's view that the ideological objective had primacy. It may indeed be that McLaurin defines 'ideology' too narrowly.

A tentative conclusion would be, therefore, that ideology in Soviet foreign policy thinking remained ultimately important at least as a defining principle. Actual 'pragmatism' and subordination of the ideological dimension (support for 'progressive against less progressive' tendencies) in the circumstances occurred partly as a consequence of *realpolitik* beyond the Soviets' control, and partly because of the flawed nature of the planning of their overall strategy, which, as designed by Kremlin officials, was often unrealistically ideological and dogmatic in its approach. But this 'pragmatism' had its place in the long-term strategy, which continued to aim at the establishment of a Soviet-allied bloc of Marxist-led states. Although by the early 1970s there was some evidence of an emerging pro-Soviet bloc, including Syria, Iraq and the People's Democratic Republic of Yemen (PDYR), ultimately this strategy was unsuccessful in the Arab world where arms sales were not enough to win support in perpetuity.

Soviet justification for its actions was liable to the criticism (not least from the Chinese) that such an interpretation of communist ideology was merely a screen to justify a foreign policy that was in reality solely based on state interests. In other words, the USSR was acting like a normal superpower, defending its own security interests and striving to maintain parity with the US. We believe that the purely 'positivist' approach – considering Soviet actions as determined solely by its interests as a superpower – does indeed offer an adequate interpretation of Soviet policies in the Middle East.

Soviet policy towards its supporters in the region changed in the mid-1980s in the light of the domestic revolution sparked by the coming to power of Mikhail Gorbachev and his programme of glasnost and perestroika. The impact of changes on the domestic front affected the conduct of foreign policy, including Soviet relations with the Middle East. The Kuwait crisis is a case in point, as Mirsky highlights: 'things began to move with the advent of the "new political thinking", particularly when "de-ideologicalisation" of foreign policy was announced. This entailed a decline of ideological priorities and "socialist" commitments abroad.'[13] It also implied a retreat from the confrontation, on all levels, with the US in the Middle East arena. This transition in Soviet thinking was well managed on all sides, particularly during 1990 and 1991 when the Gulf crisis could have threatened the new relationship that was being carved out between Moscow and Washington. US sensitivity to changes in the Soviet approach to international relations played an important part in maintaining a policy of constructive co-operation with the Kremlin.

With the Soviet Union largely absent from the Middle East did this signal a decline in conflict? In many respects one might be tempted to argue for a correlation between the end of the cold war and extension of superpower rivalry in the Middle East and the American-proclaimed decade of peace-making that characterized the 1990s. Indeed, American sponsorship of peace negotiations throughout the 1990s resulted in historical peace conferences bringing together Israel and its Arab enemies, the conclusion of a peace treaty between Jordan and Israel, and a timetable for peace nego- tiations and limited autonomy between Israel and the Palestinians. This picture of peace-making, however, does not tell the full story and American efforts must also be scrutinized in other areas of the region such as Iran, Iraq and the Maghreb. As one recent critic of US policy has noted

> today more than half the Middle Eastern landmass is without US diplomatic representation. Yet incredibly, we are asked to admire the United States political 'success' in the Middle East – and to have faith that the grotesque imbalance built into the Arab–Israeli negotiations represents a just peace.[14]

But even that comment cannot conceal the fact that after forty years of antagonism between the two superpowers, at the end of the twentieth century US influence in the Middle East faced no serious external competition. In many respects, however, such superiority over the region cut both ways. In the absence of external competition successive US administrations have only been constrained by internal political dynamics and the ways in which they have also been experienced as forms of terrorism against US targets within the region, as well as outside it. This concern was reflected, for example, in the policy of 'dual containment' that characterized the Clinton administration's policy to the Middle East. Dual containment meant a strategy of isolating Iran and Iraq as threats to Western and specifically American interests in the Middle East. It was also apparent in the personal and sustained commitment by President Clinton to achieving a peace settlement between Israel and the Palestinians. However, at the end of his tenure it seemed that such strategies had not been completely successful, especially with regard to the by then faltering MEPP, and would not be pursued by his Republican successor George W. Bush.

For the Bush administration there was little intent to overly involve itself in Middle Eastern affairs, with the exception perhaps of Iraq. Here there were a variety of voices at the US table that proposed seeking some kind of resolution to business that was not finished in 1991, resolving the eroding of international support over maintenance of the UN sanctions regime and tackling the threat posed by Saddam Hussein to US interests in the Gulf region. Events on 11 September 2001, however, changed the thinking and policy of the Bush administration almost overnight. The issue of American strategic, economic, and political interests throughout the Middle East suddenly rose to the top of the Bush administration's agenda. In this respect George W. Bush was faced with no option but to confront the Middle East as a major feature of policy-making under his administration. The attacks perpetrated by al-Qaeda on 11 September 2001 were not the first against US targets but they were in respect of targets on American sovereign territory. It underscored the consequences of hostile perceptions to US policy and its effects in the Middle East as experienced by the citizens of the region on a daily basis. In many respects the change in US policy towards the Middle East, and the means by which it addressed issues such as the Palestinian–Israeli conflict, was inevitable and has only been accelerated by a new analysis of events and their import to the region as a whole in the wake of the 9/11 attacks. The stamp of the Bush administration was always going to be apparent in a shift away from a self-defined mediator function – characterized by Clinton who sought to create a momentum in conflict resolution which he had hoped would start with Ireland and end with Israel and Palestine. In this respect Bush was never going to pick up from where Clinton left off in either theatre and this has been demonstrated in both contexts.

The US administration under Bush has consistently demonstrated a disinclination to getting 'fully involved' in progressing the conflict out of violence and into resolution/negotiation mode. In an address to the American people in Janaury 2002, following the fall of Kabul in Afghanistan and the ousting of the Taliban regime and most al-Qaeda elements, President Bush identified two states in the Middle East, Iraq and Iraq (along with North Korea) as the elements of an 'Axis of Evil', declaring 'states like these, and their terrorist allies, constitute an axis of evil, arming to threaten the peace of the world', and adding that 'Our war on terrorism has begun . . . ' This was a clear indication that the administration in Washington would now pursue a series of strategies, including a military one, against such regimes. This had enormous consequences for public opinion within the region towards the American government, and a sense of disquiet was prevalent among the leadership of ruling regimes across the region. If Bush was to be taken seriously then the war on terrorism was sure to ship up in the Middle East in the not-too-distant future. By March 2003, despite the lack of support by the UN, the USA, and its coalition partners, launched Operation Iraqi Freedom and President Bush pledged that

> the US and our allies pledged to act if the dictator did not disarm. The regime in Iraq is now learning that we keep our word. By our actions, we serve a great and just cause . . . Free nations will not sit and wait, leaving enemies free to plot another September 11th . . . And by defending our own security, we are freeing the people of Iraq from one of the cruelest regimes on Earth.

In winning the military campaign in Iraq, however, a positive outcome in terms of the objectives of American interests in the Middle East may be more difficult to achieve.

4   Generation jihad
Conflict in the name of Islam?

Hostages kidnapped and murdered in Beirut . . . Tourists murdered in
Luxor, Egypt . . . The destruction of the Twin Towers in New York . . .
Simultaneous suicide attack on the Pentagon in Washington . . . American
soldiers killed in their barracks in Saudi Arabia . . . A tour party murdered
in Yemen . . . The American Embassy bombed in Nairobi . . . Algerian
schoolgirls stabbed to death . . . Israelis bombed in street-side cafés . . . The
litany of Islamic violence from the Middle East appears limitless. The rise
of the so-called 'Green Peril' of Islamic-inspired violence and conflict
dominated newspaper headlines, television images and radio reports during
the last two decades of the twentieth century. With the end of the cold
war, the fall of the Berlin Wall and the collapse of the Soviet Union and
communism many were ready to declare Islam the new menace to global
peace and stability.

Writing in 1993 an influential American academic declared that 'Islam
and the West are on a collision course. Islam is a triple threat: political,
civilisational and demographic.'[1] For this writer, and many others like
him, the relationship between the West and Islamic civilization has always
been and will always be based on military conflict. Muslims are perceived
and portrayed as an aggressive civilization, Islam has 'bloody borders',
violence is repeatedly cited as an indiscriminate way of life against Serb,
Jew, Hindu, Buddhist and Catholic. The locus of this threat was the Middle
East and it was argued that Muslim fanatics would ensure that the region
became synonymous with conflict in a battle with the West for global
command.

Indeed much contemporary debate about the resurgence of political
Islam in the Middle East has been based on the facile assumption that Islam
itself is inherently violent and militant. Accordingly the presence of a
majority Muslim population in the countries of the region will always
lead to violence, terrorism and protracted conflict engaging jihad-minded
Mujahideen. Is this the sole explanation behind the kind of headlines so many

in the West view, hear and read about? In the latter decades of the twentieth century was Islam the most formidable threat to the stability and security of the entire region and even the entire globe? This is the fundamental question that this chapter seeks to answer.

At present a perception of permanent conflict and violence is the primary image of Islam, which influences a number of policy-makers and the media and colours common perceptions of many people in the West. Since the success of the revolution of Iran in 1979 and the establishment of the world's first Islamic republic based on rule by the Shi'a clergy, there has been a growing fear of Islam in the West. The roots of this fear of the 'other' lay in orientalist traditions that have characterized European (and later American) relations with the Middle East since the nineteenth century. Such traditions have always characterized the Arab East in a negative light and have been politically motivated by the inherent desire in the West to dominate in its relationship with the East.[2] In terms of events since 1979, and the concurrent emergence of political Islam, the West has been guilty of choosing to interpret and represent those events and processes in a limited dimension. Said puts it succinctly when he declares that in the West,

> knowledge of Islam and of Islamic peoples has generally proceeded not only from dominance and confrontation but also from cultural antipathy. Today Islam is defined negatively as that [with] which the West is radically at odds, and this tension establishes a framework radically limiting knowledge of Islam.[3]

That cultural antipathy is reflected throughout the Western media and categorized as Islamophobia through the hostile stereotyping of Muslims as terrorists and enemies; see such films as *Rules of Engagement*, *Executive Decision*, *The Seige* and *True Lies*. A regular scan of newspaper and television headlines and images regularly associates Muslims with violent depictions – holding guns, masked, and engaged in wars, intent on oppressing their own as much as outsiders, and hostile to the West. Such depictions help biased and bigoted policy-makers draw a Manichaean distinction between the Christian West and Muslim East that becomes a virtual reality through the support of such simplistic divisions in the modern media. We will argue that the construction of this view of Islam is diametrically at odds with the real relationship between faith and struggle (jihad) which continues to be important to the majority of Muslims across the globe.

On 13 March 1996 in the Egyptian resort of Sharm al-Sheikh the leaders of some thirty countries met for a half-day under the auspices of the American-convened and pretentiously titled 'summit of the peacemakers'. The meetings, speeches, photo opportunities and declarations that resulted were designed to communicate an important message to the Palestinian Islamists of Hamas and Islamic Jihad who had engaged in a series of suicide bombs in Israel that had killed sixty-one people during the previous month. In an attempt to save the beleaguered Middle East peace process, which such attacks were undermining, the 'peacemakers' declared that they were ready to wage war against the Islamists. While it can be assumed that no one seriously believed that the hastily convened half-day trip to Sharm al-Sheikh would win the so-called war against the Islamists, the 'summit of the peacemakers' left a strange impression within the international community that terrorism, particularly of the religious type, was a real threat not only to the Middle East but to the entire international order.

The attention paid to the issue of so-called Muslim or Islamic terrorism in the Middle East was highlighted by the peacemakers summit. Indeed, throughout the late 1990s many writers emerged to condemn Islam as a religion of violence, identifying a new generation of activists across the region dedicated to jihad, or what they called Holy War. As one such writer asserted, 'in Islam's war against the West and the struggle to build Islamic states at home, the end justifies the means . . . radical political Islam placed atop these societies in the Middle East has created a combustible mixture'.[4]

Does this categorization of a religion representing millions of Muslims in the Middle East adequately explain patterns of conflict across the region? Lewis believes it does, declaring that 'the Muslim world [not just the Middle East] is again seized by an intense and violent resentment of the West'.[5] Yet such sentiments stand in stark contrast to the measured tones of Egyptian President Hosni Mubarak (himself a Muslim), who remarked at the peace-makers summit that 'Muslims, like any other religion, Islam, like any other religion, is against violence, against any act of violence under any title.'

Nevertheless, the political perspective that Islam was established through the sword, that the founder of the faith Prophet Mohammed was a radical military and political leader, has sunk deep into the collective conscious-ness of Westerners. From this foundation further fear has been fuelled, particularly in America, in response to acts of terrorism such as the bombing of the World Trade Center. The American media, policy-makers and public have been alarmed at this phenomenon of terror in their own country, and more specifically they have struggled to make sense of such violence, even if little of it is actually Muslim inspired, in the post-cold war era where peace and security were supposed to be guaranteed. The current fixation with the 'Green Peril' – as the Islamist threat is referred to – has been manifested in a variety of ways. From this a fear of Islam per se has been generated.

In the Middle East itself, however, Islam and the role of Muslim populations in the conflicts of the region are perceived from a variety of standpoints rather than just one. Conflict involving Islamists – those Muslims who are politically active – is not always manifested through violence. Opponents of such Islamist activism, such as the secular Ba'athist state in Syria, have often been responsible for perpetrating the violence, the conflict and the worst atrocities. In 1982, for example, the Syrian authorities massacred 10,000 members of the Muslim Brotherhood – a Sunni reformist Muslim organization that engaged in welfare and education activities – in the town of Hama following a civil protest against the Ba'athist authorities. In a country like Lebanon, subject to fifteen years of civil war, occupation by Israel and a military presence by Syria, the breadth and diversity of Islamist views of conflict are wide. There are followers of Muslim Islamist preachers and activists, Sunni and Shi'a, who believe that change within the system is the best way to achieve Islamist-inspired goals. Indeed, for the majority of Muslims, including activists within Hizballah, there is no role for violence as a dominant motif of Islamic resistance, as interpreted according to religious law, to foreign occupation or oppression. In reality, and very much contrary to the popular perception current in the West, Islamism in the Middle East has largely played its part in opposing despotic and authoritarian rule through legitimate means, promoting civil society and a regeneration of grassroots politics. Where the state has failed to provide even the most basic of services to its people, Islamist organizations have stepped into the breach to ensure that the poorest citizens are in receipt of basic welfare support.

The resurgence of Islam and the revival of the Muslim religion in the social, economic and political life of the Middle East has been identified since the late 1960s. Such a revival or resurgence in the Muslim context, however, has been received more negatively than a revival of faith in, say, the Christian context, where evangelical movements are not perceived as a threat to any regional to international order. Instead single events such as the revolution in Iran in 1979, where Shi'a clergy led by Ayatollah Khomeini emerged dominant from the revolutionary coalition that overthrew the Shah, are represented as defining and universal moments for the entire Muslim population of the Middle East. Despite the religious, cultural and ethnic differences in a region dominated in number by Sunni Muslims, fundamentalist, anti-Western Islam as perceived in the Iranian context throughout the 1980s has been held up as representative of the nature of Islam throughout the region.

In Egypt, Jordan, Lebanon, Saudi Arabia, Algeria, Tunisia, Syria, Kuwait and even Israel, however, Islamism could be identified in each context in many guises. While it is true that conflict and associated violence often came to dominate relations between Islamists and the state, there were only a handful of examples where Islamists formed organizations or movements for specifically violent purposes. In Egypt, for example, we may find in the variety of Islamist groups – the majority of which have never engaged in acts of violence – a few whose acts of terror have grabbed the headlines and resulted in a full-scale onslaught by the state against Muslims from across the political spectrum. While in Egypt it was true to argue that in the past the institutions of Islam have supported (rather than come into conflict with) the state, the later decades of the twentieth century witnessed the emergence of a dichotomy in this respect. While Islamist groups have been active in the country since the late 1920s and tension between such groups and the state inevitable under the secular leadership of President Nasser (1952–1970), violent conflict only truly emerged from the late 1970s onwards. The establishment of radical Islamist cells whose members were influenced by thinkers such as the Egyptian Sayyid Qutb, led to violent conflict and confrontation with authority. In 1981 one such group, Jamaat al-Jihad, assassinated Nasser's successor Anwar Sadat. Such groups condemned the hostile attitude of the state to Islam, decried the government and its leadership as apostate and atheist, thus declaring that they were compelled by the laws of Islam to declare a defensive war (*jihad bis saif*). From that time such radical groups have been responsible for attacks on government institutions, the assassination of politicians, poets, authors, journalists and foreign visitors to the country. Yet, as Esposito observes, by the end of the 1990s, 'despite sporadic eruptions of violence and continued confrontation between the government and Islamist militants, in general a quiet rather than violent revolution had occurred in Egypt'.[6]

The involvement of Islamists in conflict with the Egyptian state has emerged as an important element in domestic politics since 1945. But in terms of a historical overview we would argue that the conflict was as often generated by the state in its attempts to quell the emergence of a mainstream opposition movement that engaged in legitimate protest against state corruption, anti-democratic practices and political authoritarianism against all its opponents whether Islamist or secular. It would, therefore, simply be misguided to declare that in Egypt the country's Islamic movement has been engaged in violent jihad directed at the overthrow of the state and the establishment of Islamic rule. Conflict has emerged as very much a two-sided affair. In 1992, for example, in response to extremist violence directed at state officials, Egypt's rulers ordered a security crackdown in the poverty-stricken neighbourhood of Imbaba in northern Cairo which was home to approximately 250,000 people. In early December some 15,000 police, army and intelligence officers descended on Imbaba declaring the area a no-go zone and imposed a curfew. During the curfew a campaign of mass arrest operated during which more than 800 people were arrested on suspected involvement in Islamist opposition and terror. Such a campaign proved deeply unpopular with the majority of ordinary Egyptians and was seen as further evidence of the degree to which the state and its leaders were out of touch with its citizens.

In the Israeli–Palestinian context, however, jihad (as formal resistance waged by Palestinian Islamists) against Israel had become, by the mid-1990s, yet another new but depressing facet of this particular conflict. Two Palestinian Islamist groups, Hamas and Islamic Jihad, were responsible for bombings and suicide missions against Israeli civilians. In 1996 alone hundreds of Israelis, including non-combatant women and innocent children, were killed in such attacks. These attacks were motivated by a political leadership that advocated or called for an end to Israel's occupation of Palestine through a strategy of jihad. Hamas leaders contended that conflict with Israel through other means (national armed secular-based struggle) had failed the Palestinian people in the quest for liberation from Israeli rule.

The emergence of an actively Islamist-nationalist dimension to the conflict with Israel, particularly during the Palestinian uprising (Intifada) in the late 1980s, succeeded, in some quarters, in adding a potent religious dimension to the conflict. Thus, for many young Palestinians of the refugee camps Islamist rhetoric and a return to the mosque became the primary lens through which they now viewed their enemy and interpreted the long conflict that had engulfed them. On the Israeli side the increasing manifestation of the Islamist phenomenon (which they had been partly responsible for encouraging), and the ensuing violence, had a major impact, not only on the peace process but on internal security concerns and the whole gamut of national politics. Israel's own religious radicals upped the ante, declaring they would confront the Muslim threat to Judaism.

Yet the issue of conflict through a religious campaign of violence by elements within the Palestinian camp turns on whether groups like Hamas and Islamic Jihad are innately predicated on violence and terror or whether such actions are part of a strategy in a campaign for liberation from foreign occupation for which much of the international community has also censured Israel. As such it touches upon the more philosophical debates about religion and violence, as well as armed struggle, as part of liberation movements. Hamas leaders claim they are legitimately waging a jihad against foreign occupation. Their campaign of bombs and suicide missions, however, has been called into question in an era of peacemaking when the acceptability of violence is questioned as much within the Palestinian community as outside it.

Hamas, like its predecessor the Palestinian Muslim Brotherhood, was initially established as a reform movement that did not specifically advocate violence as a means of achieving its goals. In some respects conflict with Israel was initially to be avoided while members of the movement concentrated on winning support through the well-known strategy of preaching and education. Coercing people back to the active practice of their faith in all spheres of life was not actively encouraged. By the end of the 1990s the same could not be said of the organization. By the time that the PLO and Israel signed up to a peace process and interim autonomy the Hamas movement, and its armed wing the al-Qassam Brigades, was actively pursuing jihad not just against Israel's soldiers but also against civilians, including women and children. To what extent such actions can be theologically sanctioned is highly questionable. We know of no evidence to suggest, for example, that the lives of women and children should be taken, even in a war in defence of Islam on Muslim territory occupied and ruled by a foreign power.

In Algeria, where serious civil conflict has gripped the country since the early 1990s, Islamist violence has had a major impact on the descent into chaos and the loss of many thousands of lives. Here an authoritarian secular regime has been engaged in a battle against a broad Islamist opposition movement. In addition, the conflict in Algeria is also about the impact of political liberalization or democratization on developing societies where the majority choose a path that is at odds with the economic and political reforms advocated by the international community, and where the level of assistance offered by international financial institutions such as the World Bank and major bilateral donors such as the United States is conditional on the progress of liberalization. Indeed, it should be remembered that the descent into chaos in Algeria was precipitated by a decision to halt elections – in effect put the stops on democratic process and change – as a result of foreign desire (US and French) to limit the success of Islamists at the polls. As such Algeria, in as much as it reflects the bitter decline into internal conflict involving Islamists, is also once again an example of the impact of Western perceptions of the threat posed by Islam to an international order dominated by their mores and values. Fearful of the emergence of a modern Algerian state based on the Iranian revolutionary model, the US and France used their influence to pressure the Algerian leadership into pulling the country back under the leash of military rule.[7]

The crux of the conflict is a war in which

> on the one hand the state is characterised by illegitimacy and divided by 'hawks' and 'doves'. On the other hand, Islamists with a goal of total hegemony – and who themselves are torn between 'radicals' and 'moderates' – are fighting to replace the existing regime.[8]

The contest for power in Algeria was precipitated by an economic crisis that hit hard at the population at large but cushioned a corrupt and increasingly elderly national political leadership that had rested on the tarnished laurels of independence delivered from the French in the 1960s. The vanguard of opposition against government in the 1980s, like elsewhere in the Middle East, was increasingly Islamist in orientation. The main organization, Fronte Islamique du Salut (FIS), quickly generated popular support in elections (local as well as first-round national) on an anti-establishment platform calling for the overthrow of the nationalist-dominated state and the establishment of an Islamic polity in its place. Fearing further popular gains in national elections scheduled for January 1992 the Algerian government sought to contain the Islamist 'threat' by suspending elections, declaring a state of emergency and allowing the military to effectively seize control of the state.

Since that time it has been estimated that as many as 100,000 Algerians – the majority of whom were civilians – have been killed in this horrific conflict. A plethora of Islamist groups took up arms after the state of emergency was declared. In bringing a war to the government, the majority killed in massacres, bomb attacks, executions and stabbings have been ordinary civilians rather than the national army or various branches of the police force. The military has defended itself as well as taking up the offensive through some brutal means of engagement against the Islamists. Thousands of Mujahideen have been imprisoned, tortured and killed. A litany of human rights abuses have been committed by both sides in this bloody civil war.

The religious nature of the war in Algeria has been called into question on many occasions. Amirouche, for example, has argued that 'present-day Islamist insurgents, like their nationalist predecessors [who wrenched independence from the French] seek to achieve essentially secular goals irrespective of the utterances of orators or their avowed objectives'.[9] Religion, nevertheless, has remained a potent symbol in this conflict, motivating not just a handful of discontented and megalomaniac clerics but many thousands from all walks of life in Algeria to engage in another guerrilla struggle against the state.

War-weariness, however, was certainly a factor, irrespective of other issues, in the election in spring 1999 of a new President, Abdel Aziz Boutefika, who pledged to promote national reconciliation and an end to conflict. His peace plan, backed by Algeria's generals, has included an amnesty for Islamist rebels which resulted in early 2000 in the announcement that the 8,000 strong Islamic Salvation Army, the primary guerrilla movement in the start of the civil war, would be disbanded. Those failing to sign up to the peace deal have been targeted in further military offensives on rebel hideouts and camps. While the conflict between Islamists and the state is a long way from over, it is hoped that an end to its more bloody and violent episodes may be on the horizon.

In Iran the popular revolution which overthrew the Shah in 1979 was commonly described as Islamic, thus altering the political landscape of the entire region. Even in the twenty-first century the political changes in Iran are still regarded as a signal of change in the rest of the region. The establishment of an Islamic state led by religious Shi'a clerics, notably the Ayatollah Khomeini, put a different face on many aspects of conflict within the entire region, not just in Iran itself.

A striking example is the Arab–Israeli conflict where Iran under the Shah was never perceived as a threat to Israel. All that changed with the establishment of the Islamic republic. Anti-Israeli and anti-American rhetoric was broadcast by the state-controlled media. In addition, as part of Khomeini's vision of exporting the Iranian revolutionary model, considerable support and funding were extended to those amongst the Arabs willing to subscribe to the Iranian agenda. In Lebanon the radical Shi'a movement Hizballah (Party of God) received millions of dollars from Iran in support of its guerrilla campaign against Israel which, following its invasion of 1982 to oust the PLO, remained in partial occupation of the Shi'a-dominated south of the country.

It might be argued, however, that rather than Iranian characteristics, it is the Shi'a ones of opposition, martyrdom and sacrifice that ultimately changed the emphasis or dynamics of particular conflicts across the region. It should also be remembered that the Iranian revolution and subsequent Islamic republic did not, as so many predicted, usher in an era of conflict and chaos leading to the downfall of an array of Arab regimes across the region. Two decades later Iran is one of the few examples in the region where fair elections are now a feature of the political system. In addition, the rise of reformists and their internal victory over the country's more hard-line clerics proves that the wind of change is influencing Islamism, directing it away from conflict.

To portray Islam as we have described – through the headlines and not the stories behind the headlines – is to give a false impression, both of the political spectrum that Islam in the Middle East represents and of the types of conflict which have drawn Islamist movements. Empirically, so-called Muslim terrorists remain a small and disparate group that has emerged out of a variety of political backgrounds whose power and impact among the masses have become exaggerated. Within the broad spectrum of Islamism, groups like Islamic Jihad are marginal players. In our view they do not, as Rapoport claims, represent 'the gospel for the youth', inaugurating a 'new era in Islamic thought'.[10] Instead these Islamists, who are motivated as much by spiritual impulse as by more temporal concerns in the arena of conflict, and who embrace political violence, are a tiny minority. As we mentioned earlier, the extent to which Islamist organizations choose to counter the Western construction of negative stereotypes of them is questionable. In the majority of cases any dissemination of an alternative message in Western policy-making circles is greeted with hostility. Even those Western academics writing alternative accounts of Islamist movements are labelled 'apologists for terrorism'. In the US, in particular, Muslim lobby groups which seek to counter such reductive visions of Islamism and Islam have faced a major uphill struggle, in particular in lobbying the US Congress, widely acknowledged as historically sympathetic to the pro-Israel lobby and known to influence the policy-making process in Washington. In the late 1990s attempts to promote warmer relations between the US and Iran, for example, and the breaking down of anti-Western and Islamophobic barriers, met with only mixed success and were hampered by insensitive handling, for example, of visits by high-ranking Iranian officials to the US who found themselves subject to stringent searches by immigration officials upon their arrival.

The purpose of this chapter is not to deny that acts of political violence or terrorism have perpetrated conflict by individuals who employ the symbols of religion, whether those symbols are Muslim, Jewish or Christian. Rather, it is to question whether it is the nature of specific religions themselves, Islam in particular, which is violent and conflict-driven. As Taheri asks, 'is Islam a religion of terror?'[11]

In our opinion Islam as a faith system, Islam as represented by its holy books and its preachers, is no more or less a conflict-driven religion than dimensions of contemporary Hinduism, Judaism or Christianity. In modern times the importance of faith is not that it is the cause of conflicts but rather that conflicts have assumed religious dimensions among adherents of various faiths. This is a major challenge in respect of conflict resolution, as well as the inherent challenge this poses to political orders or ideological viewpoints that are secular in foundation. In the twenty-first century Islamism is perceived as emerging in a political form that has less to do with protest politics and more to do with terrorism. Images of destruction arising from suicide bombers and from the carnage of 9/11 bolster this perception. Within that framework of understanding the concept of jihad, and the generation of young Muslims commonly associated with it, are labelled and understood as solely fixated with violence and terror. Acts of terrorism perpetrated by those understood as Muslim, who even claim to act 'in the name of Islam', acquire new meanings, new understandings and a sense of existential threat to everyone standing outside the Muslim circle. The fact that jihad, for example, within Islamic (rather than contemporary Islamist) discourse is understood in many dimensions and layers, including as a highly prescriptive, defensive act, and contains other elements as harmless as encouraging Muslims to pursue a good education, is almost entirely obscured. Religious adherents may use their religion to promote a variety of routes through life, but in this context Islam is far from being the sole reason why the Middle East tends to be a byword for conflict in the modern world. Some Islamists and their radical revolutionary messages may be one of the reasons why innocent lives have been lost and why countries like Algeria have been engulfed in so much internally generated conflict. But even in Algeria Islam or Islamism is not the sole reason for the predilection for violence. The state, as well as other political forces in Algeria, is as guilty of inflicting terror. Nevertheless, there is a real threat inherent to certain discourses of Islamism that have gripped particular constituencies in the Middle East that feeds on a culture (often created and perpetrated by the state) of brutality, totalitarianism and authoritarianism. In such contexts dimensions of Islamism become nothing more than a competitor in environments where other forms of politics are and have been absent for decades. Faced with repression and frustrated by the inability to create change peacefully, violence becomes the only expression of political power. The perceived complicity of Western states in supporting the perpetuation of such regimes undermines the philosophies of liberal democracy, open and plural governance. Thus, other, broader explanations, have to be forthcoming; explanations that include these issues alongside the politics of authoritarianism, economic and social factors and other problems that currently beset the region.

5 Sectarian conflict

Lebanon, state without a nation

The nature of the Lebanese state, which formally gained independence from the French in 1946, has been weak and precarious to say the least. The denominational system of politics and government in Lebanon has institutionalized sectarian differences between Christians and Muslims who are themselves further divided into a variety of denominations frequently at odds with each other. The sectarianism of politics has been the major factor propelling the Lebanese into conflict with each other. The savage fifteen-year-long civil war of 1975 to 1990, which left 100,000 dead, was complicated and exacerbated by the introduction of a Palestinian dimension and the consequent intrusion of two external powers, Israel and Syria, fighting their battles by proxy using allies amongst Lebanese society. With the enforced withdrawal of Israel and its surrogate militia from southern Lebanon in May 2000, against the background of some progress towards a comprehensive Middle East peace settlement, the prospects for the future stability of the country should have improved, although the domestic political system remains corrupt and flawed. Making sense out of the Lebanese tragedy and learning the lessons from this conflict is an ongoing project.

For many years Lebanon has been a classic example of a deeply divided society. There are obvious parallels with several other countries, including South Africa under apartheid, Northern Ireland and the former Yugoslavia. During the civil war Lebanese frequently killed each other for purely religious reasons. As white had killed black (and vice versa) in the old South Africa and as Protestant has killed Catholic (and vice versa) at times of seemingly mindless sectarian violence in Northern Ireland: in all three countries wider political contexts and external influences have distorted and aggravated religious, ethnic and racial divisions. Yet as many writers have pointed out, Lebanon in the 1960s was held up as an example of a country that was an oasis of calm in a troubled region. To quote Albert Hourani: 'a country which had achieved an almost miraculous balance between different

Map C – Lebanon

communities and interests, and which was enjoying political stability and peace, a comparative neutrality in the conflicts of the region, and a prosperity which seemed to be self-perpetuating'.[1] So what went wrong?

Some of the answer lies in geography and much in history. The country is mainly mountainous behind a narrow coastal strip with a society made up of communities of ancient origin.[2] For most of the nineteenth century Ottoman Imperial appointees had sought to impose order on the various ethnic and religious minorities who had traditionally sought refuge from central authority on the 'Mountain', and who jockeyed for influence elsewhere in the more accessible areas. These officials, as part of the attempts by Constantinople to centralize imperial authority, tried to extend their influence by undermining the long-standing system of feudal chiefly rule, which had held sway in the mountain fastnesses.

A significant development in the mid-nineteenth century was increasing interest and involvement in the Levant – what is now Israel, Lebanon and Syria – by the European powers, in particular France, whose self-imposed 'civilizing' mission in the region (exporting French culture and influence) involved offering protection to the Christian communities in Lebanon. France's first intervention in 1860 followed the destruction of a large number of Maronite Christian villages by their Druze rivals, allied to the Ottoman authorities. Subsequently an autonomous 'Little Lebanon' was established in the central mountains, with a Maronite majority and a Christian governor ruling with a multi-denominational council formed on a proportional basis: four Maronite, three Druze, two Greek Orthodox, one Greek Catholic, a Shi'ite and a Sunni. The Turkish authorities appointed the governor with the agreement of France and of Britain, which was also seeking a role in the area in support of its commercial interests.[3] This religiously defined balance foreshadowed the political structure of a larger modern Lebanon, and European rivalry was finally settled in favour of France during the First World War. As we have described in Chapter 2, the Anglo-French Sykes–Picot Agreement of 1916, carving up the Near East, was endorsed by the award of a mandate for Lebanon (and Syria) to France at San Remo in 1920 following the post-war dissolution of the Ottoman Empire.

Thus 'modern' Lebanon emerged as a distinct geo-political entity. It was constructed from part of the former Ottoman Greater Syria (referred to as 'Geographical Syria' in the Sykes–Picot Agreement). This new country was in effect a 'Greater Lebanon', twice as large as its 'Little' predecessor and with a more complicated sectarian diversity in which the combined Christian majority had been reduced from 79 per cent to 53 per cent of a population of just over 600,000.[4] Other new Middle Eastern countries created (or foreshadowed) by the colonial powers within artificial and unnatural frontiers at the same time as Lebanon also absorbed built-in fault lines – ethnic and religious. Israel, Turkey, Iraq and Syria are cases in point. But they could not match Lebanon's hotchpotch confessional jigsaw encompassing three significant Christian denominational divisions and three Muslim ones, plus a number of smaller Christian splinter groups.[5] A further potentially destabilizing factor was that there was no numerically dominant group forming an overwhelming proportion of the population. The difference in numbers between the three major groups, Maronite, Sunni and Shi'a, is relatively small, with no single community accounting for even half the population, as compared to some other countries with deep ethnic or religious divisions such as Cyprus, Malaysia, South Africa, India (post-partition) and the Sudan.[6] A society deeply divided into two factions is not a recipe for harmony; how much more so in Lebanon where there is so much fragmentation even within already complicated divides.

Until 1943 when they lost their influence, the French dominated the Lebanese scene as a neo-imperial power. Communal differences were deliberately reinforced by a familiar colonial ploy of divide and rule. Under the guise of a fairly structured inter-sect political system the French in effect reproduced the former confessional arrangements of the 'Little' Lebanon in the 'Greater', as if the Christians were still in a large majority. Accordingly the Francophile Christians predominated with the connivance of the mandatory authorities, and their share of the important offices of state – including the presidency – was out of proportion to their shrinking numerical superiority. (The census of 1932 estimated that the Christians constituted 51.3 per cent of the population.[7]) In consequence, almost half the population of the new Lebanon felt disempowered and many refused to work within the system. The Sunnis, a community dominated by notables educated under the former Ottoman Empire, opposed the very existence of the state. They yearned for a Pan-Syrian identity. Many of them agitated for union of Muslim-dominated areas with Syria when in 1936 the French mandatory authority recognized the principle of Syrian independence with the establishment of the Syrian Republic. Shi'ite notables tended to co-operate with the French but ordinary Shi'as were suspicious of Christian domination.

The other significant sect with Muslim origins, the Druze, also controlled by traditional chiefly families, was divided in its attitude to the government. Although disliking the Maronites, the powerful Jumblatt family, at least, was prepared to work with the French. Nor were the Christians united, with the Greek Orthodox – although concerned about Muslim rule – jealous of Catholic (Maronite) domination.

Stoten argues that the Lebanon, although a recognized state, had not, even by the end of the civil war in 1990, developed the attributes of nationhood.[8] Imported European notions of statehood, of government independent of religious affiliation, made little impact in a country composed of a heterogeneous kaleidoscope of religious groups, all of whom were determined to protect parochial political interests. As we have just discussed, this was certainly true of the Lebanon under the French mandate, where much of the population felt excluded from a share in power and trapped within a state whose boundaries seemed to ensure perpetual control by one community supported by an external power (not too far removed from the situation in Northern Ireland as perceived by the Catholic nationalist minority). In the modern era most Europeans have become used to associating themselves with nation-states rather than an exclusive religious affiliation, but in the 1990s we have witnessed a new phenomenon with the breakdown of the politics of national identity. Now many European states are experiencing the emergence of parochial nationalist and separatist tendencies (amongst them Belgium, Spain, Scotland, former Yugoslavia, former Soviet Union) and resisting supra-identity packaging within a wider European identity.

Another weakness of the Lebanese system, particularly during the mandate, which has continued to inhibit normal political development in more recent times, has been the domination by notables or small conservative elites of society. This was as true of the Christian factions such as the modern Maronite descendants of the neo-Feudal 'Lords of the Valley' as it was of the Muslims, whether under the sway of leading Druze families or their Sunni counterparts, where a handful of families tended regularly to fill the ministerial posts that came their way. The Shi'a leadership similarly came mostly from large landowning families, and all these notables, whatever their confessional background, protected their privileged positions by discouraging popular participation in the political arena. Up to 1957 40 per cent of the parliamentary seats were held by landowners. Such political parties as did emerge and were represented within Parliament were factional groupings or coalitions.[9] Ideologically motivated parties were active, but mostly outside the legislature. Even these tended to have a religiously doctrinal basis and some of the Christian parties were also influenced by the European Fascist movements of the 1930s.

Full formal independence for Lebanon in 1946 did not mark a new beginning, although it finally removed the French as players in its internal affairs. It was the National Pact of three years previously that was a more important milestone in the development of modern Lebanon. In essence the Pact was an (unwritten) constitutional arrangement accommodating sectarian differences prevalent at that time, and marked the culmination of a growing rapprochement between Maronite and Sunni elites. Although an important reference point in the short history of Lebanon, it represented in practice, as far as domestic politics were concerned, little more than fine tuning of previous sectarian power-sharing formulas between the two principal participants, with provision for participation by other religious groups.[10] Domestically it entrenched a rigid system of sharing out the three top jobs: a Christian President, a Sunni Prime Minister and a Shi'a Speaker of Parliament. The Druze, further down the pecking order, were to provide the Foreign Minister as their allotted perk. This system of government by triumvirate remained in place at the end of the twentieth century. The Pact, despite attempts by the French to retain some say in Lebanese affairs, paved the way for an independent Lebanon – this being a goal for Christians and Sunnis alike. It also represented a compromise between the Christian leadership shrugging off French tutelage and protection, and Muslim leaders turning away from Pan Arabism in accepting Lebanon as a separate entity; a country with an 'Arab appearance' as it was described at the time.[11]

Thus Lebanon entered the post-Second World War era with the same flawed sectarian and elitist dominated system, with power shared mainly between the Maronites and Sunnis, that it had experienced under the mandate. Yet from 1943 until 1975, with one hiccup in 1958, the Lebanese political system was seemingly successful in providing a basis for considerable political freedom and prosperity. Of all Middle East governments that in Beirut was the least intrusive – *laissez-faire* at its most strikingly liberal. It even largely absented itself from the educational sector; only 40 per cent of children were at government schools in 1959. Most pupils were at private religious institutions, which did nothing to help bring diverse communities together. Lebanon, with its liberalized market economy, free trade and the absence of exchange controls, became the banking centre of the Near East and one of its main commercial hubs. This apparent prosperity, however, concealed a growing division between the Christian and Sunni elites, who benefited most from this commercial and financial activity, and the urban and rural poor. Amongst this underclass were an increasing number of Shi'as who swelled the ranks of the urban working class as the rural economy declined. The Lebanon, under its predominantly Christian leadership, also sought to isolate the country from the tensions of the region, turning its back on crisis in the Arab World brought about by the Arab–Israeli conflict, although the country became reluctant host to 150,000 Palestinian refugees after the 1948 war. The events of 1958, however, demonstrated that it was not possible to keep the world at bay indefinitely.

The 1958 crisis was at one level just another indication of the struggle for influence between Lebanese elitist factions, and was eventually solved in the same way as earlier inter-confessional confrontations by means of an adjustment of ministerial posts to include groups previously excluded. But its main significance was a reflection of growing popular opposition to Maronite ascendancy from mostly Muslim factions united in demonstrating the disenchantment of the urban poor at not sharing in the country's apparent prosperity. The international dimension was also important, as this widespread popular opposition was also a protest against the government's perceived empathy with Western policies in the region. The Maronite leadership's embrace of the American Eisenhower doctrine (see Chapter 3) and its opposition to any manifestation of Pan Arabism as demonstrated by its refusal to join inter Arab unions – whether with Egypt and Syria or Jordan and Iraq – were interpreted as sympathy for the West. But President Nasser's calls for Arab unity struck a popular chord throughout Lebanon, chiefly amongst the urban masses who resented and were ashamed of their Christian politicians' attempts to hold Lebanon aloof from the main stream of Arab politics. Additional popular ferment was engendered by the overthrow of the Hashemite monarchy in Iraq, perceived to be Western-leaning and opposed to Nasser's strident Pan Arabism. The army refused or felt unable to put down the disturbances, and it took the despatch of US Marines to Beirut at President Sham'un's request to restore order. The crisis was contained, but two new elements in Lebanese politics – the activities of the urban poor and the influence and involvement of external actors actively being enlisted by rival internal factions – were to threaten the Lebanese political system and eventually lead to its disruption and the destruction of much of Lebanon itself.

With the benefit of hindsight we can see that the Lebanese civil war, which erupted in 1975, had its seeds sown in the disturbances of 1958 which, in their turn, had graphically illustrated the depth of the fault lines in Lebanese society. Superficially Lebanon continued on a path of comparative political freedom and vigorous commercial activity based on the same principles that had guided its development in the immediate post-war years; power sharing between the main religious communities, the deliberate restriction of state control and, as Yapp put it, 'a tacit concern to set on one side the unresolved conflict about the nature of Lebanon – how much was it Arab and how much distinctively Lebanese'.[12]

Much has been written about the causes of Lebanon's tragic and bloody civil war. Was it mostly an internal phenomenon, another challenge to Maronite dominance by other factions within the Lebanese body politic? Or was it caused primarily by external factors brought about by the presence of Palestinians on Lebanese soil, which sucked Lebanon into the wider Arab–Israeli conflict? Most commentators agree that the spark that ignited the fifteen-year confrontation was the clashes in April 1975 between Christian Phalangist forces and Palestinian fighters in which the mainly Muslim and Pan Arab Lebanese National Movement supporters weighed in on the side of the Palestinians. This led remorselessly to a general free-for-all, with the collapse of the government, the disintegration of the army and widespread conflict, which had the character of a monolithically (if only superficially accurate) Christian versus Muslim confrontation.

There is no doubt that the presence of the Palestinians in the Lebanon since the 1967 war had been largely disruptive to the stability of the country. The refugee population had swollen to over 300,000 and had become thoroughly politicized, especially following the arrival in 1971 of the PLO leadership and a large number of fighters after their expulsion from Jordan. But even before that the Lebanese government had been drawn into a confrontation with Israel that they had wished to avoid, as they had been unable to prevent Palestinian commandos using southern Lebanon as a launch pad for raids into Israel. Indeed, as early as 1969 the Lebanese government had lost control of much of the south of their country to the Palestinian guerrillas. By this time the area was known as 'Fatah Land' where the Palestinians, with the support of much of the Arab world, had virtually set up a state within a state as they had also tried to do in Jordan. All this invited Israeli retaliation as much against Lebanese as Palestinian targets in a vain attempt to pressurize the Lebanese into controlling guerrilla activities, a tactic the Israelis were still using up to the time of their withdrawal from Lebanon twenty-two years later.

The Palestinian dimension, and by extension the dynamics of the Arab–Israel dispute, cast a long shadow within Lebanon and became a major, if not the major, ingredient in exacerbating and prolonging internal conflict, feeding on the inherent instability of Lebanese society with its sectarian fault lines and dysfunctional government. A 'normal' and more 'natural' state could have coped with the Palestinian presence and its external ramifications. But the regime, a major section of whose leadership was emotionally divorced from the region and its problems and which probably yearned for a return to the cocooned security of a Maronite-dominated 'Little Lebanon', had no answer to forces unleashed by years of sectarian-based misrule and rampant Arab nationalism. Under pressure the Sunni–Maronite consensual partnership fell apart. Indeed it fell at the first fence; fatally split on the issue of how to deal with the Palestinians, with the Christians looking for a military solution which they could not get any significant Sunni leader to endorse. Not surprising perhaps, given the difficulty of deploying an army with mostly Christian officers and a mainly Muslim rank and file against a movement enjoying considerable popular Muslim support inside and outside the country. All this against the background of probable Syrian military intervention on behalf of Palestinian and local radical Pan Arab and Muslim factions. Not surprisingly, the Lebanese government found itself paralysed by indecision and inhibited by gloomy forebodings of likely obstacles, most of which turned out be self-fulfilling prophecies as Lebanon fell apart.

The main features of the civil war make horrific reading.[13] From 1975 onwards, with a few periods of remission and respite, Lebanon was engulfed in an expanding maelstrom of bloodletting and destruction. Inexorably, outside powers – the Syrians, the Israelis, Iran, the West and the UN – got sucked into a quagmire of Lebanese inter-factional turmoil compounded by external intervention. Lebanon became a major battleground within the wider issue of Arab–Israel confrontation. Syria, either through direct military involvement with stationing of troops in the country or via proxy groups such as the Shi'a Amal and various Palestinian militias, pursued its quarrel with Israel. At the same time the presence of several thousand Syrian regular soldiers increasingly limited the freedom of action of the Lebanese government itself.

The Israelis – via a policy of aggressive retaliation against Palestinian attacks, then partial occupation and eventually, in 1982, invasion – sought to destroy or neutralize the Palestinians and their radical Arab supporters represented in southern Lebanon. They were also concerned to neutralize the threat presented by the stationing of Syrian missile batteries and other heavy weapons in the country. This was also part of a broader strategy of carrying the fight to their Arab opponents, which included the formal annexation of the Golan Heights captured from Syria in the 1967 war. With the support of their Christian Phalangist allies they besieged and bombarded Beirut and forced 140,000 Palestinian refugees to flee South Lebanon for the security of the Syrian controlled Beqaa valley. One of the most horrific incidents of this time was the massacre in 1982 of about 2,000 non-combatant Palestinians, including women and children, in the refugee camps of Shatilla and Sabra by Christian Phalangist militia uninhibited by the presence of their Israeli allies who had surrounded the camps as part of an anti 'terrorist' search-and-destroy operation.

Under international pressure the Israelis partially withdrew from the country, maintaining their occupation south of the Litani river, which they also tried to protect with their local surrogates – most notably the South Lebanon Army (SLA), a Christian militia which they had trained and armed. The Israelis were not averse to arming other groups irrespective of confessional allegiance as local circumstances permitted, only to find their arms subsequently used against them. The SLA were then bogged down in a fierce local war with Druze fighters, which led to southern Lebanon being effectively partitioned between warring factions. The Palestinians, battered by the Israelis, were themselves factionally divided, and the struggle for control of the leadership led to more heavy fighting and to the expulsion of the PLO leader Yasser Arafat and 4,000 fighters from the Lebanon. Attempts to re-establish a PLO presence in the Lebanon were strongly opposed by the Syrians who used their local allies in Amal against Palestinian supporters of Arafat, adding yet another dimension to the internecine conflict.

With constant inter-factional conflict – Christians against Muslims, Sunni versus Shi'a – the emergence of such ruthless organizations as Islamic Jihad, and the excesses of bloodthirsty militia from all sects, Lebanon became synonymous with mindless violence, senseless sectarian killing and widespread destruction. The kidnapping of a number of Westerners by radical Islamic groups reinforced the negative image the civil war created in the world media and international opinion. The city and countryside were cantonized. At the height of the civil war Lebanon split up into seven separate areas, each under the local control of one of the various militias. In Beirut the 'Green Line' divided the Christians from the Muslims. On both sides of it the capital lay in ruins. The Lebanese army had long ceased to function; commerce was at a standstill, the banking community had fled and inward investment had dried up. Ceasefires and fine-tuning the confessional balance within the government proved to be short-term and ineffectual palliatives. One episode of multi-national military intervention in 1983 by a 6,000 strong US/French/Italian force to try and stabilize the situation following the Israeli withdrawal ended in failure, with heavy American and French casualties. This multi-national deployment was perceived by the radical Muslim groups to be one-sided in its support for the Christian-led government. After this bloody rebuff for international peacekeeping it seemed to many in the international community that Lebanon was terminally dysfunctional and probably beyond help.

By late 1990 the 1989 Taif agreement had led to the end of the internal conflict after the failure of a Pax Syriana to restore order, following fierce fighting between Amal and the Iranian-influenced and financed Hizballah. Exhaustion and successful Arab mediation were the major factors. Indeed this was a notable achievement for persistent and imaginative Arab diplomacy, in striking contrast to attempts to find 'Arab solutions' to other conflicts; the Gulf crisis of 1990 to 1991 was to be a case in point. The contentious continued presence of Syrian forces in Lebanon was taken out of the hands of the Lebanese politicians during these negotiations and put to one side, awaiting agreement between the two governments – but not before several hundred more people had been killed in fighting between the rump of the Lebanese army, led by a Christian general, and Syrian forces stationed in Lebanon. Attempts to replace the Syrians with a multi-national Arab force failed because of Syrian opposition. Inter-sectarian face was saved via a Charter of National Conciliation, part of which involved the enlargement of the national assembly with seats, for the first time, equally divided between Christians and Muslims. Implementation of the Charter proved troublesome and met with principally Christian opposition to what they saw as the further erosion of their privileged positions. But at last the civil war was effectively at an end.

The last decade of the twentieth century was an era of some hope for Lebanon, if not one of unbounded optimism. Stability of a sort was restored and large-scale reconstruction of central Beirut began. By 1992 all the Western hostages had been released, an indication of a return to something like normality in the Lebanese political scene. The Lebanese–Syrian security treaty of 1991 formalized the position of Syrian troops in Lebanon, and Damascus continues to call the important shots in the formulation of Lebanese policy. Lebanon thus enjoys the security benefits of a Pax Syriana but at the expense of significant restrictions on its room for manoeuvre. Now in the new millennium, the success of Hizballah in forcing an Israeli total withdrawal from its self-styled security zone, and the rout of its proxy South Lebanon Army, has brought peace to the south. Lebanon has been largely freed from the fear of massive Israeli retaliation for attacks launched by Hizballah, on the pattern of the 1996 Israeli assault on Kana. At last there is a prospect of government control being reasserted in the south that has for so long been ruled by militias. The death of President Assad and his son's succession to the Syrian presidency bring hope of a less one-sided relationship with Damascus. The ordinary Lebanese Muslims, as well as Christians, are increasingly resenting the obtrusive heavy hand of their neighbour, although some of the more radical elements still see the Syrians as their protectors of last resort.

Optimism needs to be qualified. The Lebanese political system is still fundamentally sectarian. Rule by triumvirate reflects a discredited and outmoded formula based on a deliberately fudged assessment of the country's demographic realities. Any new census would undoubtedly show the extent of the numerical superiority of non-Christians (see note 5). It still endorses and systemizes sectarian division. Cracks are papered over but the basic fault lines remain. Elections, because of gerrymandering and manipulation, are an inaccurate test of public opinion and not just because of the inflexibility imposed by sectarian straitjackets. The old familiar power-brokers continue to flex their financial muscles as they did in the elections of August/September 2000, demonstrating the ability of big business to purchase electoral support. And even if the institutions are made genuinely sound, as Luciani and Salamé have pointed out,[14] 'it must be recognised that the formal existence of democratic institutions in no way guarantees per se that a segmented society will be able to achieve political unity and evolve towards integration'. The fundamental question of what Lebanon is – a legitimate Arab state with a regional role or something different – has yet to be settled to the satisfaction of many of its people, especially the Christian minority. The wounds of the savage civil war remain unhealed for many and, as in South Africa and Northern Ireland, cross-community bridge building and reconciliation are the urgent priorities. But when a government is so blatantly sectarian it is unlikely to heal the divisions that perpetuate its very existence.

The Palestinian refugees[15] are still there, dispossessed, wretchedly poor and unwanted. There has never been an attempt to integrate them into Lebanon nor does it seem likely that there will be a serious effort to do so. Their future largely depends on events beyond Lebanese control and the progress of the Middle East peace process. Recent developments can hardly be encouraging. In the absence of a comprehensive settlement the Palestinians remain a ticking time bomb. How they and their supporters behave will also determine the Israeli attitude to Lebanon. Another connected issue is the future of Hizballah and Amal. Will they (and their paymasters) be content to act purely as Lebanese political parties? Prolonged stalemate or events elsewhere in the region might induce them to return to a more provocative anti-Israeli policy, using southern Lebanon as their launch pad with or without the consent of the Lebanese authorities. The long-term Lebanon–Syria relationship is also a hostage to the fortunes of peacemaking. The Syrians will also need to decide if it is safe to lift the Pax Syriana and trust the Lebanon to manage its affairs in a way that is not detrimental to Syrian interests: most importantly the stability of the Western Levant. Whilst Lebanon remains a deeply divided society, with a flawed power structure reflecting these divisions, this may be a risk that Syria is just not prepared to take. The new regime, headed by the young President Bashar Assad, shows no sign of taking it. Especially so, as following the removal of Saddam's regime Washington has turned its sights onto Damascus as a 'sponsor of terrorism' – the government's alleged support for Hizballah in particular being the main basis for this accusation. Under this pressure the Syrians will wish to maintain a grip on its clients in Lebanon in case any of those factions opposing the Syrian presence take their cue from Washington and seek, once again, to destabilize this so easily troubled state.

6 Ethnic conflict

The forgotten Kurds

Under the banner of Arab nationalism and other unitary ideologies, ethnic-based claims to political and other rights in the Middle East have been suppressed. As a result, as the Kurdish question illustrates, ethnic conflict is a very real issue in the post-world wars era. The arbitrary nature of state creation following the collapse of the Ottoman Empire and the emergence of regimes striving to consolidate and maintain their authority within highly artificial borders has forced issues of ethnic identity underground without eradicating them. It has been the response by states to the pressures imposed by a growing ethnic and national consciousness amongst the Kurdish people that has brought about episodes of sustained conflict within three countries in the region.

The Kurds, who number at least 26 million,[1] are, after the Arabs, the largest ethnic group in the near and Middle East. About 90 per cent of the total Kurdish population world-wide live within the boundaries of one Arab country (Iraq) and two non-Arab states (Turkey and Iran). The remainder are found in Syria (about one million), the former Soviet Union (half a million) with 700,000 living in a wider diaspora. Despite their numbers the Kurds have consistently been denied the right to statehood[2] and have been a persecuted minority in the region. Kurdish demands for self-determination have for nearly a century led to conflict, particularly in Iraq, Iran and Turkey. The conflict has been both horizontal and vertical in dimension; within the Kurdish communities and between the Kurds and the state. Additionally individual states have exploited Kurdish ambitions in order to promote tension or conflict with their neighbours. With increasingly little hope of establishing statehood or achieving secession from any of the states within the region they have encountered armed repression in response to their attempts to obtain formal recognition of their claims for political and civil rights. The states' response to such demands, particularly in Turkey and Iraq, has resulted in policies of enforced population transfer at one end of the scale of state-organized oppression to ethnic cleansing and wholesale massacre

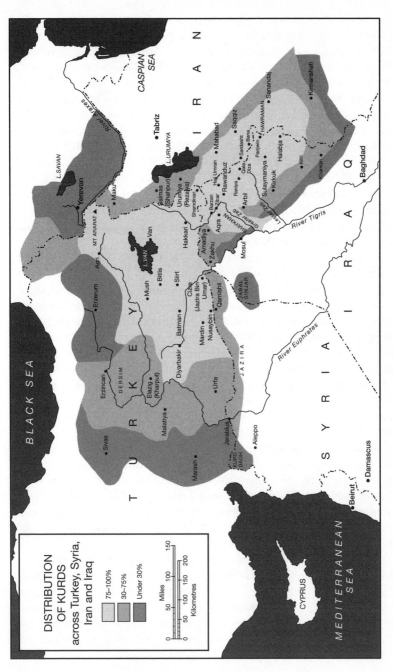

Map D – Distribution of the Kurds across Turkey, Syria, Iran and Iraq

at the other. In this chapter we will examine why this is so and look at the prospects for the Kurds in the opening decades of the third millennium.

The Kurds are descendants of Indo-European tribes (including Turkic, Armenian and Assyrian) who settled in the Zagros Mountains at various intervals, most numerously during the second millennium BC. This area, which is still the heartland of their main population concentration, is the mountain range where Iran, Iraq and Turkey meet. The region is not exclusively Kurdish but Kurds form a significant majority in most of it. The name 'Kurdistan' was applied to this area as early as the thirteenth century AD. Later, in the sixteenth century, after the Kurds, via a number of tribal migrations, had moved north and west onto the Anatolian plateau, the term 'Kurdistan' became a common way of denoting a system of Kurdish chief-doms or minor principalities. It appeared on a few maps, its boundaries were imprecise, but, as McDowell has pointed out, it is more than a geographical term as it also refers to a human culture that exists in that region: 'To this extent Kurdistan is a social and political concept.'[3]

Divisions amongst the Kurds have over the past century frustrated attempts to achieve unity or indeed work towards any form of effective political mobilization. They lack a single systemized language, either spoken or written. Some dialects are incomprehensible to other Kurds, although many Kurds can understand one of the two major dialects. Nor are Kurds religiously homogeneous. The great majority are Sunnis but at least three million living in Anatolian Kurdistan are Alevis, an unorthodox form of Shi'ism. Some other Kurds in Iran are also Shi'a. The Kurdish 'nation' also includes smaller sects such as the Yazidis and Christian minorities like the Assyrians and Syrian Orthodox. In some countries Kurds appear to suffer from something of an identity crisis.[4] Tribal differences, the remoteness of many of their communities and the ambitions and influence of the traditional local leaders (the Aghas) have also been an obstacle to Kurdish unity.

The first stirrings of Kurdish nationalism, in a modern sense, probably began in the early twentieth century at the time of the revolution in Constantinople in 1908 led by the Young Turks. Their ideals of constitutional reform and representative government struck a chord with educated people within the Ottoman Empire, the Kurds being no exception. But Kurdish nationalists in their newly formed urban clubs and societies were not united and failed to attract the support of the rurally based *Aghas* who saw such movements as a threat to their position as the traditional community leaders. At any rate the whole process was undermined by the declaration of war in October 1914 by the Ottomans on the Allies. In the ensuing hostilities the Kurds were used by the Ottomans to play an ignoble part through their involvement in comprehensive ethnic cleansing, amounting to genocide, of Armenians in Anatolia.

The defeat of the Ottomans by the Allies in 1918 ushered a whole new order into the region by the victorious European colonial powers. The old empire was dismembered and artificial new states within frontiers that took little account of pre-existing tribal and ethnic boundaries were created in the former Arab regions of the empire at the instigation of the British and French. Their ambitions were partly tempered by the American President Woodrow Wilson with his idealistic and unrealistic Fourteen Point Programme for World Peace. Point twelve affirmed that non-Turkish minorities of the former Ottoman Empire should be 'assured of an absolute unmolested opportunity of autonomous development'. This came too late to help the massacred Armenians but presented the Kurds with a brief and transient possibility of embryonic statehood.

But it was not to be. This ethnic group was not at a state of development that would equip them to rise to the challenge of post-war nationalism and seize the fleeting opportunity of benefiting from the precipitous creation of nation-states. The fact was that the benefits of change seemed unclear to most Kurds. National consciousness hardly existed outside the confines of urban intellectual circles. Traditional tribal loyalties, rather than national ambitions, influenced village or pastoral Kurds in their mountain retreats. Here the *Aghas* held sway, wary of any attempt by urban 'progressives' to undermine their positions – suspicious also of neighbouring tribal leaders and unwilling to contemplate making common cause with old rivals for the nebulous and uncertain goal of a Kurdish ethnic entity. The status quo and its familiar security probably appealed to such conservative people who would anyhow feel remote and insulated from the dramatic changes taking place in the outside world.

For these reasons the provisions of the Treaty of Sèvres in August 1920 proved historically inopportune to the Kurdish people. At a later stage they would surely have welcomed the autonomy it envisaged for the predominantly Kurdish areas of Turkey and British-controlled Mosul (now in Iraq), with a view to eventual full independence. Many Kurds now regard the Treaty of Sèvres as a sadly missed opportunity. But even if there had been an effective nationalistic Kurdish leadership at that time to pursue statehood, such an effort would almost certainly have been nullified by the revolt of the Turkish revolutionary leader Kamal Ataturk. In the name of a new unified Turkish state he repudiated the Ottoman government's signature of the Treaty of Sèvres. Most Kurdish leaders, influenced by religious rather than nationalistic sentiments, willingly supported Ataturk's revolt, which they saw as protecting their Muslim identity against threats from the Greek Christian forces that had invaded Turkey from the west and the Armenians (and Soviets) from the east.[5]

The Treaty of Lausanne in July 1923 tidied up issues left unfinished by the failure to implement Sèvres. Turkey's sovereignty over territory seized by Ataturk – including all of Anatolia – was accepted and Britain's suggestion that Turkey should recognize the Kurds as a 'national minority' was rejected. Although apparently Ataturk considered autonomy[6] for the Kurds that same year, it was never mentioned or discussed publicly. At any rate nothing came of it and thus prepared the ground for confrontation between the Turkish government and Kurdish nationalists. We look further at the Kurds and the growth of Kurdish nationalism in modern Turkey later in this chapter. We now examine very briefly the modern history of the Kurds, against the background of events following the First World War, within the three countries where the vast majority of the community is to be found.

Iran: elusive independence

Over six million Kurds make up about 10 per cent of the population of Iran, which has also other significant ethnic minorities: Arab, Turkic and Baluchi. Kurds probably have more affinity culturally and linguistically with Iranians than with Arabs or Turks. Nevertheless, their relationship with the government in Tehran has not been a happy one, although not characterized by the same degree of consistent oppression and brutality as has been their experience in Turkey. Iranian Kurds have, generally speaking, been allowed to propagate their culture and to speak their language, but any attempt to advocate separatism has been severely dealt with.

Reza Shah, who came to power in Iran after the First World War, was the first of the 'Persian' monarchs for many years to attempt a policy of firm centralization. His immediate predecessors had only been able to exercise varying degrees of control over their territory. As with the Ottoman Empire, the hand of governmental authority often lay very lightly on the more remote regions. In these circumstances the Kurdish tribal chieftains enjoyed considerable local autonomy, often acting on behalf of the central government as the regional authority. Reza Shah changed all that as he sought to subjugate the tribes, including forcibly resettling nomadic ones, which he managed to do by the 1930s. Tribal chiefs in most cases made the transition to landowners – although stripped of civic position but retaining influence with their traditional tribal followers.

At the end of the Second World War about a third of Iran's Kurds experienced a fleeting moment of independence. Britain had occupied Western Iran in 1941 to counter Reza Shah's perceived pro-German tendencies. At the same time the Soviet Union also intervened in an area of strategic interest to it. With the Soviet Union's prompting, the Kurds living in north-west Iran, under the nationalist leadership of the Kurdistan

Democratic Party of Iran (KDPI), declared an independent republic, as separately did the Azerbaijanis within the same region. The Kurdish entity called itself the Republic of Mahabad. Due to its small size it failed to attract many Kurds from other areas, either to join with it or to offer any support against government forces that re-established control following the Soviet withdrawal. Nor was there any support from Moscow, who dumped the Kurds having cynically used them as a lever with their government. As with the Turkish Kurds at the time of Sèvres, the majority of the Iranian Kurdish tribal community was not motivated by nationalism and the infant republic lacked enough popular inter-tribal and international backing to secure its survival. Indeed, some of the government troops who reoccupied the abortive republic were themselves Kurds from elsewhere in Iran, thus demonstrating how narrow was the appeal of Kurdish nationalism at that time.

The Kurdish experience under the last Shah of Iran and the successor regime of the Islamic republic continued to be an unhappy one. A small number of militant nationalists went underground following the dismantling of their republic and remained so for most of the Shah's reign. The majority of Kurdish areas stayed under martial law as the Iranian regime was determined to suppress any movement that might threaten the unity and cohesion of the state. The new factor was growing Iraq–Iran inter-state confrontation and conflict as described in Chapter 7. In the late 1960s, having taken refuge in Iraq, KDPI activists launched armed resistance against their government from Iraqi territory. Ironically their activities were largely frustrated by Iraqi Kurds led by Mustafa Barzani, at the behest of the Tehran regime, which was at that time actively supporting an Iraqi Kurdish rebellion against Baghdad. This anti-KDPI activity by Barzani was doubly ironic as he and 3,000 of his Iraqi Kurdish followers had fought for the short-lived Mahabad Republic against the Shah barely twenty years previously! This was a striking example, which was continually to bedevil pan-Kurdish ambitions, of the inability of the separate Kurdish leaderships in Iraq and Iran to agree a common cross-frontier policy. For both leaderships the overriding imperative was to seek autonomy within the state structure rather than to seek common cause with their tribal neighbours. As the Shah's land reforms had destroyed the economic power of the *Agha* large landowners, 'Kurdistan' itself remained underdeveloped and impoverished in comparison with the rest of Iran, at the very periphery of the Shah's economic revolution.

Another opportunity for achieving a measure of autonomy for Kurds in Iran was not seized in the early chaotic days of the Islamic republic. A movement led by some of the tribal chiefs to break away from state control was not supported by the KDPI who, as a sophisticated urban party, opposed tribalism and regarded the rural Kurds as reactionaries. Moreover, a significant Shi'a minority amongst the Kurds supported the Ayatollah Khomeini's regime as being a Shi'a revolution and therefore objected to the policies of separatism espoused by the majority Sunni Kurds. In addition, the new regime strongly opposed any move towards autonomy by the ethnic minorities for fear of national disintegration at a time of great upheaval. Some Kurds living near the Iraqi borders took advantage of the 1980s war with Iraq to achieve very short-lived local independence following Iraqi successes in the land war. But after the ceasefire the central government was quickly able to restore its authority throughout the Kurdish areas. Since then the position of Iranian Kurds has greatly improved in terms of enjoying civil rights. They are, for instance, fairly represented in the Islamic republic's largely democratic institutions. But any dream of a separate politically autonomous entity seems as remote as ever.

Iraq: brutality and ethnic cleansing

Modern Iraq was a British creation. Its establishment followed the capture of Mesopotamia from the Ottoman Turks in 1918. In determining the extent of the territory of the new state the British were uncertain what to do with the mostly mountainous Kurdistani regions lying to the north and east, but also including the major ethnically mixed town of Kirkuk dominated by a Kurdish hinterland. Post-war the immediate interest of the British was, at minimum cost and involvement, a desire to pacify the population living in the mountains of Kurdistan so as to remove the threat that their inhabitants posed to the strategically vital Mesopotamian plain. As in Turkey and Iran, the Kurds were divided and unable to agree a common strategy. Some looked for incorporation into the new Iraq, soon to be ruled by the British-appointed Hashemite King Feisal. Others, led by Sheikh Mahmud Barzinji, strove for some kind of independent entity free of foreign control, although initially happy to accept British protection. There were many who preferred to unite with those Kurds now in Turkey with whom they had close cultural and linguistic ties. And probably a majority of the *Aghas* would have been content to further local ambitions within the kind of *de facto* autonomy their ancestors had enjoyed in the old Ottoman Empire.

In the end the British yielded to pressure both from Turkey and from their client king in Baghdad. The Turks resisted any autonomous arrangement for Iraqi Kurds, which they feared would have dangerous implications for the status of 'their' Kurdish community, whose separate ethnic and cultural identity they were seeking to deny. King Feisal of Iraq needed to incorporate the Kurds of southern Kurdistan into his kingdom so as to ensure a Sunni majority in what otherwise would be a largely Shi'a state. From the beginning he had relied upon the support of the Sunnis, who made up the majority of people in central Iraq, including the major landowners around Baghdad. He used Sunnis to fill senior positions in his administration and in the military. By contrast, southern Iraq was overwhelmingly Shi'a and potentially hostile to a Sunni-led regime. Control of all the Kurdish areas was also important to the economic viability of this new country, with the prospect of the Kirkuk region producing large amounts of oil. Accordingly the British arranged for the former Ottoman province of Mosul to became part of Iraq. Subsequently the Anglo-Iraqi treaty of 1930 conferred full independence on the kingdom and omitted any of the specific safeguards related to the preservation of a minimal Kurdish separate identity as a 'recognized minority' in their areas as the British had previously undertaken in agreement with the League of Nations.[7]

Newly independent Iraq never achieved a good working relationship with its Kurdish community. Baghdad's aggressive and insensitive handling of what were primarily inter-tribal disorders provoked the growth of a more nationalist form of opposition to the regime by Kurds led by Mullah Mustafa Barzani. Barzani's nationalist fervour was also fired by the creation of the short-lived Republic of Mahabad in neighbouring Iran, which he had (vainly) helped to defend. But, as elsewhere, the Kurdish leaders could not agree on a common strategy. Many of the *Aghas* preferred to co-operate with the regime rather than confront it, and Barzani himself split his own party by making a deal with the government in 1964, condemned as a sell-out by his main critic Jalal Talabani. This split remained the basis for the continuing bitter rivalry between the two principal Kurdish political parties, the Barzani-led Kurdish Democratic Party (KDP) and the Talabani-controlled Patriotic Union of Kurdistan (PUK). As happened in Iran the Iraqi Kurdish leadership exploited Iraq–Iran hostility to further its aims, co-operating actively with Tehran during periods of conflict between the two regimes.

Since the coming to power of Saddam Hussein in Baghdad the Kurds of Iraq have paid a dreadful price for their opposition to the regime, and especially for their opportunist alliances with the Iranians. Armed conflict with the regime in 1974 to 1975 ended in defeat for Barzani's *peshmergas*[8] after Saddam had struck a deal with Iran over the Shatt al-Arab (see Chapter 7). With Iranian support now withdrawn, Barzani was powerless to prevent 500 Kurdish villages being razed and 600,000 villagers forcibly resettled by the Baghdad regime. This 'pacification' was followed by an offer of limited autonomy, rejected by the Kurdish leadership as being too restrictive. But the Iraqi leader's real savagery was reserved for the closing stages of his war against Iran in 1988, when he took his revenge for the Kurdish military alliance with his enemies. The well-documented chemical attack on Halabja in 1988 and similar assaults during the 'Anfal' operation may have cost as many as 200,000 Kurdish lives, with whole areas being 'cleansed'. Thus Saddam resorted to ethnic cleansing well before this phenomenon, as practised by other ruthless leaders, became all too familiar in Bosnia a decade later.[9] Following his defeat in Desert Storm, and with his forces routed in Kuwait, Saddam faced a spontaneous Kurdish revolt in the north, whilst the Shi'a rose in the south (see Chapter 8). This he partially suppressed with great difficulty, but continued Iraqi attacks on the Kurds led three Western members of the allied coalition, the US, Britain and France, to impose a safe haven in northern Iraq (north of the thirty-sixth Parallel). This enclave, protected by allied air power – including an air exclusion zone – and with some UN personnel on the ground, remained in existence at the start of the new millennium. Thus the Iraqi Kurdish problem was 'internationalized' and allowed a considerable number of Kurds to enjoy a large measure of *de facto* autonomy, including a National Assembly. But unfortunately the two main parties, who share most of the Assembly seats, have not entirely abandoned old rivalries, and have intermittently engaged in fierce internecine conflict.

In the late 1990s the two main parties started to work more closely together and this greater unity of purpose served the Kurds well when coalition forces invaded Iraq in March 2003. It was mainly Kurdish fighters (with US air support) who were instrumental in capturing both Kirkuk and Mosul in April. Under US pressure the Kurdish troops subsequently withdrew into their *de facto* autonomous areas. This followed threats from Turkey to intervene if the Kurds were permitted to hold on to these towns and the nearby oilfields. No way will Turkey countenance the possibility of a viable and economically self-sufficient Kurdish autonomous structure which could eventually develop into a sovereign state. Such an outcome would be a beacon for the Turkish Kurds and a powerful incentive for them either to seek to unite with their Iraqi brethren or seek a similar degree of autonomy for themselves. It will be interesting to see how the post-Saddam Iraqi government will cope with the Kurdish issue and to what extent this resurgent and long-forgotten people can find an acceptable *modus vivendi* with Baghdad. We suspect that a federal-type arrangement, leaving the Kurds with a large measure of self-government, will have be contrived as it will be difficult to persuade the Kurds to accept anything that leaves them less in control of their own affairs than is the case at present.

The Kurds in Turkey: the invisible people

As in Iraq the story of the Kurds in Turkey is one of conflict and oppression. But at least in Iraq there has been an offer of autonomy and official recognition of a separate Kurdish identity (albeit grudging and tactical), while in Turkey it was possible up to 1987 for a senior Turkish minister to ask 'Is there such a thing as a Kurd?'[10] The 13 million or so Kurds in Turkey form over 20 per cent of the population. Kamal Ataturk's aggressive policy of Turkish nationalism shut out any hope of Kurdish autonomy or even recognition of a separate non-Turkish cultural identity. Ataturk's modernizing secularism challenged the ideological basis of Kurdish belief in a Muslim state for which Kurds had fought alongside the Turks against the Greek and Armenian threat. From the beginning of their modern state-hood the Turkish authorities were desperate to promote a new homogenized identity for a new 'Turkish' nation. Hence a policy of ethnic cleansing by denial of any claim by the Kurds for a separate ethnic or political existence. In consequence all public vestiges of Kurdish identity were banned, including schools, associations and publications. Not surprisingly there were spontaneous Kurdish revolts in 1925 and 1928, which were ruthlessly crushed with many thousands of non-combatants killed. Subsequently large-scale deportations from Kurdish areas were enforced in an attempt to assimilate the Kurds into the Turkish population. The Kurdish language was made illegal and the Kurds were officially referred to as 'mountain Turks', thus denying their ethnic identity; at the same time, as non-Turks ethnically they were classified as second class citizens.[11]

Although such brutal repression kept Kurdish nationalism under control for many years, there was a powerful revival from the 1960s onwards. As in Iraq, repression failed to quench the spirits of the Kurds; rather it had the opposite effect, encouraging a rise in militant nationalism, as all other paths of self-expression seemed blocked by an obdurate state. Denied their own political parties, the Kurds united with Turkish leftist groups and gained, albeit indirectly, a political presence in the body politic. But it was a surge in radical extremism that was to hold centre stage. Right-wing reaction throughout the 1960s and 1970s had led to further massacres and prepared the way for the appearance in 1984 of the previously unknown extremist Partiya Karkari Kurdistan (Kurdistan Workers Party – PKK) under the leadership of Abdulla Ocalan. Its goal has been an independent Marxist-style Kurdish state entirely divorced from Turkey and incorporating other ethnic Kurds, especially from Syria and Iraq. In the single-minded pursuit of its ambitions an organization quite as ruthless as is its Turkish opponent has evolved. Deploying a skilful guerrilla force it has also been as savage in dealing with fellow Kurds perceived as supporters of the regime (such as landowners) as with the armed forces of the state. Like the Iraqi Kurdish nationalists it has gone outside the state in search of support and refuge. In its case the ties with Syria have been close and alleged Syrian support for the PKK has brought Turkey and Syria close to armed conflict.

After a decade of bloody conflict, with the state vying with its Iraqi neighbour in adopting measures of population transfer not far removed from ethnic cleansing, there was one crucial success for the Turkish government. The capture and trial in 1999 of the charismatic PKK leader Ocalan has for the moment blunted the armed struggle as the organization agreed a ceasefire, declared publicly by Ocalan himself from the dock. But as we discuss below, Turkish Kurds will be encouraged by the success of their kinsmen in neighbouring Iraq as the Saddam regime crumbled in March/April 2003.

One positive development in the last decade has been a softening of the attitude of inflexible non-recognition of a specifically 'Kurdish' issue by the Turkish government. Under pressure from the obvious popular support for the aims (if not the methods) of the PKK, senior Turkish figures have been more willing than hitherto to consider a political solution, at least as far as recognizing, somewhat tentatively, a separate Kurdish culture. Kurdish can now be used for many purposes, including publications – but not for formal education or broadcasting. However, persecution and harassment continues; the Kurds are effectively prevented (by administrative device) from organized political activity and the community at large has remained highly politicized and anti-government. They are also impoverished, with high rates of unemployment. Moreover, thanks to the activities of the PKK, strong anti-Kurdish sentiments run high amongst ordinary Turks; the capture of Ocalan was hailed as a major victory and calls for his execution were widespread. But a growing number of Turks are calling for a political solution. European governments looking at Turkey's candidature to join the European Union may be able to moderate the regime's behaviour, making demands for a marked improvement in the country's human rights record. Time will tell if these influences bear fruit.

A meaningful measure of *de jure* autonomy looks an unlikely early prospect for two of the three major Kurdish communities we have discussed, and this bodes ill for the future of the diaspora as a whole. It seems improbable that either the Turkish or Iranian government will do more than allow a separate cultural identity to be established and maintained. Turkey, a candidate for European Union membership, is under pressure on its human rights record and will need to adopt a more enlightened attitude to its ethnic minorities if it is to satisfy its many critics in Europe. European politicians have to take account of the views of a significant number of Kurds; many of them highly militant, forming part of a Kurdish Diaspora scattered throughout the European Union. This is, however, unlikely to amount to autonomy for Kurdistan, but it may eventually lead to an improvement in the establishment of institutions reflecting a separate Kurdish identity. And of course the new factor is the major role played by the Iraqi Kurds in supporting the US-led coalition's successful removal of the Saddam regime.

If they are rewarded by continuing to enjoy a wide measure of autonomy within Iraq this will encourage their Turkish counterparts to agitate for similar treatment. This could also become embroiled in the negotiations with Brussels as a matter of human rights.

In Iran, even a liberal reforming regime will still be conscious of the dangers of ethnic disintegration if the central authority of Tehran is loosened. The Islamic regimes have inherited from their monarchist predecessors the feeling that this remains a real and present danger. As for Iraq, all will depend on the events of the next few years as a new Iraqi regime arises from the ashes of the old. A democratic and federal administration will need to bring about the conditions that will allow the coming to terms with the Kurds on a mutually satisfactory basis. The existing offer of autonomy made by the regime in the 1970s could still be a blueprint for an arrangement acceptable to the Kurds. But it would need an unprecedented level of mutual trust to be established between Baghdad and the northern provinces; no easy task given the horrific bloodletting of the past two decades when Saddam called the shots. It would also need – and this applies equally to Turkey and Iran – a united Kurdish leadership to evolve in order to represent effectively the interests of the various Kurdish communities without, it must be hoped, resorting once again to the self-defeating and divisive option of armed struggle. A federal solution in Iraq could offer the prospect of maintaining the territorial integrity of the state and democratic rights for the Kurds that could be emulated elsewhere. The demands of the Kurdish people, however, will not fade with the demise of the Ba'thist regime and future administrators should remain cognizant of this fact.

7 War in the Gulf

Iran and Iraq 1980–1989

It is tempting to portray the Iraq–Iran conflict predominantly in terms of a recent manifestation of a historical enmity between the Arabs and the Persians. Or, and indeed as well, a religious and political struggle between Sunni and Shia. But both descriptions are misleading and incomplete. This was a thoroughly modern inter-state war for thoroughly modern reasons of national interest and regional hegemony in which ideology, ethnic rivalries and religious fervour played their part but were not central to the main issues.

The war itself was also modern in its nature in terms of armaments and *matériel*: missiles, aerial bombardment and the use of weapons of mass destruction. While neither country had a nuclear capability they deployed lethal-enough chemical weapons to cause thousands of deaths and casualties. Estimates vary, but probably up to one million people were killed or injured in this decade-long conflict – 60 per cent sustained by Iran. The war also cost US$200 billion directly and another $1,000 billion indirectly, according to most estimates. By the end of the war each side had more than 1.3 million under arms – one half of Iraqis and one-sixth of Iranians of military age.[1] Both sides somewhat stretched the definition of 'military age', using young teenager conscripts and equally immature 'volunteers' as cannon fodder, especially in the later stages of the conflict.

As Yapp has pointed out, although the Iraq–Iran war has generally been known as the Gulf War, the Gulf itself, whether prefixed as 'Arab' or 'Persian', was neither the bone of contention nor the main theatre of operations.[2] We have stuck to the usual description because from the perception of non-combatants, especially the Gulf monarchies and the superpowers, the Gulf itself was the major focus of concern wherever the main fighting actually took place. As we describe later, worries about the effect of hostilities (attacks on shipping and mining) on the flow of oil and other trade through and from the Gulf (from where one-sixth of the West's oil imports originated) made external involvement inevitable – as did fears that the

Iranians were intent on 'exporting' their revolution via the subversion of minority Shia communities in Gulf Co-operation Council (GCC) countries, in addition to other considerations to do with maintaining the stability and security of the region.

It is difficult to identify a single *casus belli*, unless it was simple Iraqi miscalculation. There were points of friction aplenty between the two countries. From the overthrow of the Hashemite monarchy in Baghdad in 1958, up to the collapse of the Shah's rule in 1979, relations between the two regimes had rarely been better than correct, and often much worse. Republican, self-styled revolutionary, anti-Western Iraq was instinctively chalk to the cheese of the equally self-styled 'Imperial' Iran, westward leaning and perceived to be Washington's natural partner if not its client state in the northern Gulf. This mutual antagonism was compounded by rival ambitions for political and economic hegemony in the region. The Iranians, even unprompted by Washington, saw themselves as the guardians of Gulf security following an announcement in 1968 of the British withdrawal in 1971. This Iran considered necessary to safeguard oil exports and offshore oil installations. By contrast Iraq cast itself as the principal proponent of the concept of the 'Arab' Gulf. The Iranians, although not Arab, were more akin in political ethos to the traditional, also Western-aligned Arab Gulf monarchies than was republican Iraq – an Arab 'brother' but an uncomfortably big one.

The Iranians had demonstrated their military reach as a regional power by sending troops to Oman in 1972 to assist the Sultan in suppressing a nationalist revolt. The Iranians had also alienated much of the Arab world a year previously by seizing two strategic islands (the Greater and Lesser Tunbs) off the coast of the UAE and had imposed control on a third – Abu Musa – extracting a joint sovereignty agreement with the ruler of Sharjah through *force majeure*. Baghdad had led the anti-Iranian pack on that occasion (breaking relations with Tehran) and stridently opposed foreign intervention in Oman. But whatever the rhetoric, and despite the evidence of Iranian aggrandisement, the Arab Gulf monarchies continued throughout the 1970s to be instinctively more comfortable with Iran than with Iraq. The latter, with its radical posture on Arab–Israel in an attempt to take over Arab leadership from Egypt and its close ties with the Soviet Union (despite the regime's advocacy of non-alignment) on whom it mostly relied for arms, alienated the moderates and conservatives in the area. They of course had vivid memories of Iraq's aggressive stance towards Kuwait in 1961 when the newly independent Emirate had come under threat of attack from General Qasim's regime.

Territory became the major issue for dispute between Iraq and its Iranian neighbours from the early 1960s. The important Shatt al-Arab waterway

Map E – Iran/Iraq and the Northern Gulf

(from the confluence of the Tigris and Euphrates to the Gulf) had been under Iraqi control since a treaty of 1937 placed the border on the Iranian eastern bank low watermark. In 1969 Iran defied Iraqi instructions by using warships to escort Iranian flagged vessels in the Shatt asserting a claim, by dint of *force majeure*, to a right of navigation along the *thalweg* – the middle of the deepest shipping channel. Iran's military superiority at the time forced a humiliated Iraq to accept *de facto* use of the waterway by Iranian ships.

Further aggravation was inevitable, especially against the background of substantial Iranian assistance for Iraqi Kurds in the north in revolt against Baghdad – going on intermittently since the early 1960s – which nearly led to an all-out military confrontation following a series of border skirmishes.[3] It was during this period that both countries, realizing the vulnerability of installations in the Shatt to hostile acts, took strenuous action to relocate strategic facilities such as oil terminals away from this narrow waterway. This was easier for Iran, with its long length of eastern Gulf coast, than for Iraq, with its limited access to open sea. Consequently Iran built ports in the Gulf to lessen dependence on its principal oil terminal Abadan whilst the Iraqis sought to use overland pipelines to export their oil away from the Gulf area. This was not altogether a successful strategy as the trans-Syrian pipeline was subject to intermittent closure because of internal political upheaval. Pipelines built later across Saudi Arabia (TAPLINE) and Turkey in the 1980s during the Gulf war proved more reliable until put out of commission following the Iraqi invasion of Kuwait in 1990.

The 1975 Algiers Agreement between Iran and Iraq demarcated the border along the *thalweg*. In exchange for getting their way on the border the Iranians stopped assistance to the rebellious Kurds, who accepted a ceasefire and agreed a truce with Baghdad. Although the Treaty led to a suspension of hostilities and a lessening of the tension, the Iraqis never really accepted the *thalweg* as a *de jure* frontier and a return to control of the waterway as enshrined in the 1937 agreement remained a vital Iraqi objective.

The Iranian revolution of 1979 under the leadership of Ayatollah Khomenei started the countdown to conflict. The downfall of the Shah more or less coincided with the emergence of Saddam Hussein as President of Iraq and chairman of the ruling Ba'ath party's Revolutionary Command Council (RCC). Saddam, as Secretary-General of the party, had pulled most of the strings from behind the scenes for several years but now felt the need to entrench his position in the public eye. He immediately claimed the unearthing of an attempted coup in which he alleged that the Syrians were implicated. This led to a ruthless purge of opponents within the RCC and an abrupt end to recently formulated plans for a union with Syria, thus once again reopening the long-standing rift with the other wing of the Ba'ath party which had ruled in Damascus for several years. Saddam also cracked down on the Iraqi Communist Party (ICP) and distanced himself from the Soviet Union (and dependence on Russian weapons), whose invasion of Afghanistan in late 1979 he publicly condemned.[4] This indicated a tilt to the West, a tactic which was to benefit him during the coming conflict with Iran.

Relations between Saddam's Iraq and Khomeini's Iran deteriorated rapidly. The Iraq Sunni leadership of a predominantly secular state was concerned that the appeal of Shi'ite revolutionary Iran (exporting the revolution it was soon to be called) might inflame anti-regime sentiments amongst Iraq's Shia majority, estimated at 55 per cent of the population. The Iraqi Shi's, since the formation of the modern state, had perceived themselves as something of an oppressed majority – second-class citizens under-represented in the government hierarchy and within the senior ranks of the armed forces. There were therefore ample long-standing grievances within the community, which could be exploited by aggressive co-religionists advocating resistance to Sunni oppression throughout the region.

In an increasingly hostile war of words both the Iraqi and Iranian leaderships exchanged accusation and counter-accusation linked to territorial claims. Iraq, as part of its bid for recognition as the paramount power in the Gulf, called for the liberation of the Tunbs and Abu Musa. Tehran blamed Baghdad for demands by the majority Arab community in Iran's province of Khuzestan for autonomy (called 'Arabistan' by Arabs). Border incidents proliferated once again and Saddam Hussein probably calculated that revolutionary post-Pahlavi Iran was in such turmoil, and with its army weakened by purges, that it would not be able to resist a massive attack, albeit one confined to achieving limited territorial gains along Iraq's south-eastern border. Thus he could reverse the humiliation of conceding to Iran over the Shatt at Algiers and, using captured territory as a bargaining counter, make border adjustments in Iraq's favour to other disputed areas, including winning concessions over Khuzestan, thus demonstrating that Iraq not Iran was the power to be reckoned with in the Gulf. The overthrow of Khomeini, if not the main war objective (as some writers have claimed[5]), would certainly be a welcome bonus.

Whatever Saddam Hussein's intentions, once open conflict erupted it was soon evident that he had badly miscalculated the effectiveness of the Iranian response. The initial invasion was launched on 22 September 1980 on a 300-mile front. This had been preceded by a formal Iraqi abrogation of the Algiers Agreement on the pretext that Iran had failed to make a border readjustment as agreed at Algiers in 1975. Despite considerable early territorial gains in the south-east, much fiercer than expected Iranian resistance ensured that the war soon stopped the Iraqi advance. Indeed in spring 1982 an Iranian counter-offensive regained most of the territory occupied by Iraqi troops, including the recapture of Khorramshahr in May. Both sides were now deadlocked into an immobile war of attrition.

The Iraqi leadership had rightly estimated that the Iranian armed forces had been seriously disrupted by purges immediately following Khomeini's assumption of power. But against all expectations they managed quickly to reorganize and fight back. Saddam Hussein had given an ideological spin to his campaign by naming it the 'Battle of Qadisiyya', recalling the Arab victory over Sassanid Iran (and its subsequent conversion to Islam) in AD 637. But the Iranians more effectively summoned up past spirits of deeply rooted hostile and equally ideological images of Arab Sunnis who had oppressed Persian Shi'ites for centuries.[6] Saddam Hussein had also underestimated Khomeini's ability to unite and inspire his people to resist and defeat Iraqi aggression: motivating his troops with religious and nationalistic fervour. As the war progressed there were many eyewitness accounts contrasting the often suicidal fanatical Iranian soldiers, apparently eager to die in battle in human wave attacks, with the more conventional tactics of the obviously less-committed Iraqis. By June 1982 it was clear to Saddam Hussein that the new Battle of Qadissiya had failed. He recognized this by pulling his forces out of what little territory in Iran still lay under Iraqi control. Indeed, it was apparent to some observers even at this early stage that this war would not be decided on the battlefield.

Space does not permit a blow-by-blow chronological account of the next seven years of ultimately futile war.[7] But there are features and distinct phases worth detailing briefly. Iraq was on the defensive in the land war from 1982 onwards. By contrast Iran had succeeded in occupying nearly 300 square miles of Iraqi territory by October 1983. Indeed, until the last stages of the war Iran had much the better of land engagements, capturing Fao in 1986. In no real danger of defeat, the Iranians doggedly stuck to their apparently immutable position of no peace negotiations in the absence of massive reparations, admission of guilt by the Iraqis and the removal of Saddam Hussein from the Iraqi leadership. This obliged Iraq to embark on a policy of seeking to inflict such unacceptable damage on the enemy that the regime would be forced to the negotiating table. From 1984 onwards Iraq used its superior air power, including, from 1984, the most sophisticated French-supplied Super Etendard fighters and Exocet missiles to target Iran's petroleum export industry. Previously both sides had used missiles to attack each other's towns in what became known as 'the war of the cities'. Iraq also declared an exclusion zone in the northern Gulf and attacked vessels going to and from the main Iranian terminal at Kharg Island and thus succeeded in making the export of Iranian oil hazardous and expensive.

Saddam also sought to 'internationalize' the conflict and attract as much external support as possible. In this he was assisted by increasing Iranian intransigence in refusing to negotiate a settlement, brushing aside numerous attempts by the UN and others to mediate. Before the war the regime had courted financial backers amongst the Gulf states such as Kuwait and Saudi Arabia, arguing that Iraq would act as a first line of defence against any threat posed by Shi'a militants in Tehran. Aware of their own uneasy relations with the native Shi'a populations in their own states, the rulers of both countries were prepared to be generous with financial support for Baghdad throughout the war: loans of over US$6 billion in the case of Kuwait. Saudi Arabia was even more generous, and both states sold oil on behalf of Iraq. By the end of the conflict some estimates puts Baghdad's total indebtedness to Kuwait at $15 billion and to Saudi Arabia a staggering $34 billion! Other Arab Gulf states also chipped in with the United Arab Emirates (UAE) being especially forthcoming. With Iraq's Gulf ports like Basra and Umm Qasr under threat, its neighbours helped with opening up land transit routes for oil exports. Aqaba, in Jordan, became, in effect, Iraq's largest seaport. Generally speaking Arab countries were solid in their backing for Baghdad. Egypt's strong support (some of her troops fighting alongside the Iraqis) did much to restore her position in the Arab world following her ostracism after Camp David. Only maverick Libya and anti-Saddam Syria refrained from any form of support for their Arab brother.

As the conflict dragged on the two superpowers were also inclined towards Iraq. The US initially found both regimes repugnant and tended to remain aloof. Its attitude to Iran was particularily strongly coloured by the humiliation of the seizure of the US Embassy in 1979 and the subsequent failure of a military operation to rescue the staff held hostage. Despite strains in the relationship over Baghdad's treatment of the ICP, the Soviets were instinctively inclined to support a long-standing client. Nevertheless, both superpowers had a common concern: the effect of an Iranian victory on the stability of the region. Any 'export' of what was perceived as a subversive form of aggressive Islamic 'fundamentalism' not only had the potential to inflame Shi'ite minorities (a majority in Bahrain) in GCC countries but also to excite Islamic communities in nearby regions of the Soviet Empire. The USSR accordingly became, once again, the principal arms supplier to Iraq. European states such as France and Britain also benefited from satisfying Iraqi arms demands. The People's Republic of China (PRC) was another major weapons provider – to both sides, but more to Iraq.[8] We shall describe below how the superpowers and their allies became more directly involved in the protection of their interests as the area of conflict expanded.

Iran experienced considerable problems both militarily and diplomatically. The lack of air power and enough modern armour prevented a successful frontal assault towards central Iraq. Its ability to stir up Iraqi Kurds was initially inhibited by fear of repercussions on its own Kurdish community should the Iraqis retaliate similarly, although this was a card that was played in desperation in the latter part of the war. Thus Iran concentrated her efforts on the south where she hoped (vainly as it happened) Shi'ite Iraqis might join in – capturing Fao, cutting on occasion the main Basra to Baghdad road, but never managing to seize Basra itself. Here too the land war remained in stalemate, sapping the morale of her forces, although at one time (1986) it seemed possible that the Iranians might win a major victory in the south.

Iran's other option was to follow Iraq's example and attack shipping in the Gulf belonging to (or using ports of) states sympathetic to Iraq. Kuwait was a particular target – between October 1986 and April 1987 fifteen ships going to and from Kuwait were attacked and in some cases cargoes seized. To these maritime attacks were added the occasional (if haphazard) launch of a Chinese-supplied Silkworm missile targeted on Kuwait City. Iran also made liberal use of mines in the narrow sea-lanes of the Straits of Hormuz. Much of this activity proved self-defeating. The Kuwaitis cleverly manipulated the major powers into protecting her oil tankers, either by having them re-flagged with the Stars and Stripes in the case of eleven vessels or with the British colours for four more. Other tankers were leased from the USSR and remained Soviet-flagged vessels. Thus external parties were obliged to provide protection for their 'own' ships. A Western naval presence was anyhow in place to try to maintain normal commercial activity, deterring both Iraq and Iran, and minesweepers became increasingly involved in keeping the sea-lanes open. This multi-national task force (US, UK and France mainly), known as 'the Armilla Patrol', was a substantial naval presence by the end of the war and seen by the Iranians as mostly directed against them. The Iranians threatened retaliation and promised to sink US warships if provoked. But ironically it was the Iraqis who succeeded in attacking a US frigate, USS *Stark*, killing thirty-seven sailors. The Iraqis claimed the attack was an 'error' and apologized, but suspicions remain that it was in retaliation following media revelations that Washington had secretly supplied arms to Iran – the so-called 'Irangate' affair.[9] There were also press allegations that the US had supplied false intelligence to both sides to ensure a stalemate in the war: the argument being that it suited Washington's strategic interests to have Iraq and Iran at each other's throats so as to counter any threat that both regimes might otherwise present to the Gulf monarchies.

There were various attempts at mediation throughout the war. The UN had managed the odd success, such as brokering a cessation of attacks on civilian targets by both sides in June 1984. This, however, was subsequently ignored by Iraq, which resumed air attacks in March 1985 having been frustrated by continued stalemate on the ground. Further unilateral suspensions offered by Iraq to induce Iran to negotiate failed to achieve the desired result. Other attempts to bring Iran to peace talks continued to founder on Iranian insistence on unacceptable conditions, claiming $350 billion war reparations at one point. This attitude increased Iran's international isolation, limiting her diplomatic options; but pariah status did not seem to influence (or worry) the regime. Then Security Council action took on a new urgency with the prospect of the US being drawn into a direct military confrontation with Iran over Tehran's threats to attack US warships in the Gulf if 'provoked'. Attacks on vessels in the Gulf by both sides escalated sharply throughout 1987. The damaging of a US frigate by a mine allegedly laid by Iran resulted in a US retaliatory attack on an Iranian naval base. Security Council Resolution (SCR) 598, adopted unanimously on 29 July 1987, called for an immediate ceasefire, withdrawal of forces to international borders, and sought Iranian and Iraqi co-operation in seeking a settlement. Iraqi acceptance (conditional on Iranian agreement) was negated by Iran's condemnation of the resolution as unfair as Iraq was not identified as the aggressor and because of continued US naval presence in Gulf as 'Iraq's ally'.

Iran continued to resist pressure from the international community to accept SCR 598 and agree to a ceasefire, presumably because the regime felt that the war could yet be won. Then the tide of battle turned in favour of Iraq. Iran had enjoyed some success in the land war in early 1987, penetrating Iraqi territory in several places along the 1,200-kilometre war front. However, by early 1988 Iraqi counter-offensives causing heavy casualties (the Iraqis, in particular, making effective use of chemical weapons such as mustard gas) took their toll on an increasingly war-weary Iranian military infrastructure. Volunteers were not coming forward as before and there was apparently disagreement over strategy and tactics in the higher echelons of the Iranian government. A Kurdish offensive (the largest since 1974/75) hoping to exploit Iraq's involvement on a broad front and in support of Iranian forces, although initially successful came to a tragic end with an Iraqi chemical attack on Halabja in March 1988, killing 4,000 Kurdish civilians. Many more were allegedly killed by poison gas in a subsequent campaign after the Gulf conflict had apparently ended.[10] With their forces in retreat on most fronts, and with Iraqis on Iranian soil for the first time for some years, the Iranians unexpectedly announced their unconditional acceptance of SCR 598 on 18 July 1988. (This was shortly after a US warship accidentally shot down an Iranian civilian airliner, killing 270 people.) A ceasefire came into effect a month later. Apart from a few minor alarums and excursions the Iraq–Iran war was at an end.

The Iraqis declared themselves the victor in the contest. Certainly they had had the best of the last few months of fighting, liberating all their territory and occupying parts of Iran. But in truth this wretched war, the greatest inter-state conflict in the second half of the twentieth century, ended as a draw. Most of the goals were own ones. In terms of casualties, damage (to fifty large towns or cities) and bleeding of resources, both countries were the losers. Said Aburish called it 'an aimless war'.[11] 'Pointless' is perhaps a more fitting epithet. Saddam, preoccupied with Kuwait in August 1990, quietly conceded all points of difference with Iran in August 1990 in seeking a formal peace with the old enemy. He thus tacitly acknowledged that Iraq had achieved none of its war aims. Neither side had established a clear hegemony in the region. The international community – the UN and the major powers – had only just managed to contain the conflagration within acceptable limits; the stability of the rest of the region was maintained and a temporary loss of oil production managed without disruption to the market. But they had failed to halt it until the combatants were themselves prepared to call it quits, thus demonstrating the limitations on international intervention even when both superpowers were, more or less, pulling in the same direction. However, it has to be said, for reasons we describe in Chapter 3, that the Soviet Union was beginning its withdrawal from substantial involvement in international issues towards the end of the 1980s; they were therefore not major players in the Gulf for the latter part of the conflict.

The longevity of the conflict was primarily down to the determination and stubbornness of the two main protagonists, Saddam Hussein and Ayatollah Khomeini. Neither was prepared to give way and both managed to gain and retain sufficient control to ensure they got their way. Despite the evident futility of the war, especially as it appeared to foreign observers, the position of neither leader was seriously threatened by the indecisive outcome of the conflict. Indeed, for some years the war against old enemies was popular enough in both countries. Small successes could be presented domestically as major national triumphs. The ebb and flow of contest gave both nations hope of ultimate victory from time to time. It also suited both regimes to have an external enemy to take people's minds of domestic discontents. Moreover, as the war dragged on and became bogged down, both leaderships probably hesitated at calling a halt to hostilities, given the difficulty of explaining to their people how so much effort and bloodshed had achieved so little. Especially so as the casualties mounted; very few families in either country were left personally untouched by the carnage of war. But, in the final analysis, public opinion counted for little in both countries. And even if one of the two protagonists had clearly been seen to be the loser it is unlikely that the defeated regime would have been swept away, so efficient (and ruthless) were the mechanisms of repression. This applied equally to

Iraq since Saddam Hussein became president and to Iran following the revolution. In the latter case the Islamic republic effectively adapted and refined the instruments of control invented by the Shah.

Throughout the war both regimes felt they were playing for big stakes. Each saw the other as a formidable obstacle to their ambitions. Khomeini remained intent on the export of his revolutionary ideals via co-religionists down the Gulf. Saddam's desire for his regional hegemony to be recognized and his position in the wider Arab world appreciated drove him on. Both leaders glimpsed fleeting opportunities of victory; Iran in the land battle, Saddam via the air war. This helped to keep them going. Saddam also felt that the apparent support of the international community, with both superpowers more hostile to Iran, might in the end be decisive. Ultimately, as stalemate set in, both leaderships recognized that the chances of decisive victory were illusory and that there were limits, even in autocracies, to what could be expected of exhausted and demoralized armed forces. Moreover, both economies were badly damaged by nearly ten years of conflict. Although Saddam may have been tempted to carry on when his army started to get the better of the land war in the dying months of the war he probably was reluctant to push his troops much further. So in the end grim determination and the mutual personal hatred that motivated both leaders were just not enough for one to see off the other.

One conflict spawned the origins of a second. Iraq, with the damage done to her economy and with fears about the long-term effects that this might have on popular support for a regime somewhat dented by the war, needed a quick fix to its problems. This at least seemed Saddam's perception. How important a factor this was as a cause of Gulf War, Part Two – the Iraqi invasion of Kuwait – we will discuss in the next chapter.

8   The Kuwait crisis
Brother versus brother

The Iraqi invasion of Kuwait began in the early hours of 2 August 1990 and ended after a few hours of sporadic fighting with the occupation of the entire Emirate by 100,000 troops. This was the start of a crisis that was to lead to conflict and the comprehensive rout of the Iraqi occupying forces six months later – but only after the putting together of a massive military coalition, over 700,000 strong, under United States leadership with contributions from over thirty countries, ten of them Arab. Never before in the history of the region had so many Arab countries gone into battle against an Arab brother, one who not much more than a year previously had enjoyed widespread fraternal support against the Iranian enemy. Never before had the United Nations authorized the use of force against a member state with the consenting votes of both superpowers. A decade later, even divisions in the Arab world opened or exacerbated by this conflict remained largely intact. The United States had no serious international challenger within the region; and Iraq, still under Saddam Hussein, remained a pariah state, subject since 1990 to the most draconian sanctions regime in the history of the United Nations.

The complex circumstances surrounding Saddam Hussein's second serious miscalculation in a decade – his invasion of Iran in 1980 being the first – need to be examined in the wider international context.[1] As we described in Chapter 3, the start of the 1990s saw a dramatic decline in Soviet influence and involvement in the Middle East. President Gorbachev's twin policies of glasnost (greater openness and a measure of democratization) and perestroika (restructuring and liberalizing the economy) – the so-called 'new thinking' – started a process of loosening the grip of Moscow over the Soviet Empire, a process that was to reach its inevitable conclusion under his successor Boris Yeltsin.[2] Soviet preoccupation with domestic upheaval and the need to encourage economic assistance from the West led to a scaling down of cold war rhetoric and a willingness (opposed by old style hard-liners within the Soviet leadership) to seek co-operation rather

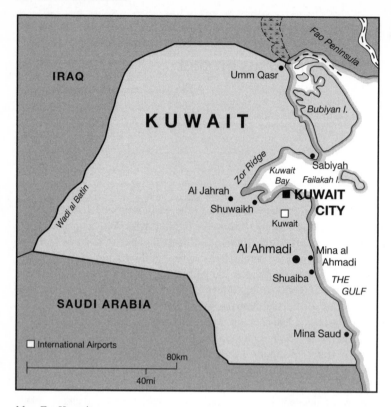

Map F – Kuwait

than confrontation with the United States. Following the Soviet disengagement from Afghanistan in 1988, Moscow, although still maintaining big power pretensions, became increasingly reluctant to take on new foreign commitments and was, indeed, unable to honour existing ones. This partial withdrawal from the world stage had serious implications for former traditional clients in the Middle East. Syria, Iraq, South Yemen and the PLO in particular could no longer look to the Soviet Union for economic and military aid, nor, as time went on, for effective diplomatic support.

   The United States and its allies were also absorbed by developments within Eastern Europe throughout the first half of 1990, as influenced by evidence of dramatic change in Moscow. Despite political and economic turmoil within the Soviet Union and the increasingly obvious and seemingly inevitable decline of Soviet influence, Washington was not yet in a position to proclaim the existence of a 'new world order' – a now hackneyed expression referring to a structure of international politics dominated by one major global player instead of two. But as Soviet power waned within the Middle East there were signs of Washington preparing to fill an impending vacuum through new contacts with Moscow's former 'clients', such as the PLO leadership and Syria. This in preparation for a new attempt to kick-start the peace process, once again in abeyance against the backcloth of the Palestinian Intifada described in Chapter 2. Not all Arabs welcomed the relentless rise of American influence at the expense of Soviet involvement. Many believed that Israel would be the main regional beneficiary of Washington's peace-brokering which, with the eclipse of the USSR and the end of bi-polarity, could operate unchallenged by any other international player, thus leading to the imposition of an unjust settlement on the Palestinians and their Arab supporters.

The Kuwait crisis has probably become the most analysed conflict in recent history, about which it has been remarked that more ink than blood has been spilt. One recurring theme in academic discourses is that contemporary observers, especially governmental ones, should have anticipated the invasion.[3] Surely, given Saddam's record of precipitate aggression and his rhetoric in the early months of 1990, Iraqi military action against the Emirate was inevitable. But despite the proliferation of hints and (with the benefit of hindsight) fairly strong indications, most people were taken by surprise. We need to discuss briefly why this was so.

As described in the previous chapter, Saddam and his regime ended their pointless war against Iran as the self-proclaimed victor. But in truth Iraq had ended a close contest marginally ahead on points. Iraq had been bankrupted by the conflict and for much of the period was largely dependent on very generous assistance from the Arab Gulf states, especially Saudi Arabia and Kuwait.[4] Iraq's pretensions as a regional superpower had foundered on the rock of Iranian opposition. There had been considerable popular internal opposition to a military adventure that had brought no measurable benefits to the country; certainly little enough to compensate for the nationwide distress caused by thousands of casualties, considerable war damage and the crippling of the economy. Saddam, although pursuing plans to liberalize the political system partly to encourage more involvement by the Shi'as and to open up the economy, remained totally dependent on the support of an entrenched oligarchy and the regime's instruments of state oppression to keep in power. He survived at least one serious coup attempt between the end of the Iraq–Iran war and the 1990 invasion of Kuwait and, despite his brutal crushing of the Kurdish separatists from 1988 to 1989, Saddam realized that further trouble from that quarter was only a matter of time.

Unabashed by his failure to have his neighbours recognize Iraqi hegemony as the dominant regional power, Saddam began to strut on a bigger stage, seeking the leadership of the radical pack in the Arab world. There followed vehement and strident attacks on Israel, coupled with a war of words with the US culminating in a resolution by the US Congress to impose sanctions on Baghdad because of Iraqi plans to manufacture weapons of mass destruction, including chemical weapons as used against Iran and the Kurds. Saddam encouraged the external PLO leadership (based in Tunis) to look upon him as a major patron and to establish an important regional office in Baghdad. He also exploited Iraq's membership of the Arab Co-operation Council (ACC) – a four-country grouping of Jordan, Egypt, Yemen and Iraq established in February 1989. Saddam used this platform to play to a wider Arab audience, turning up the volume on his anti-Israeli rhetoric and simultaneously seeking to outflank his long-standing Ba'athist rivals in Damascus who had themselves for many years been predominant radicals.

Alarm bells started ringing in the Gulf and in the West when the extent of Iraq's crash rearmament programme became apparent in 1989 and early 1990. Despite severe economic problems exacerbated by depressed oil prices, the regime was spending vast sums of money on the purchase of sophisticated weapon systems, mainly from France and the USSR, and also seeking to acquire the technology to develop an in-house capability to produce its own. The Israelis in particular had expressed concern[5] about Iraq's nuclear potential, and its ability to produce and use chemical weapons was well documented. The regime's arrest and execution of an Iranian-British investigative journalist[6] drew international attention to the existence of advanced armament-manufacturing facilities in Iraq, as did the interception of sophisticated items of technology from Western companies thought to be integral to the development of sophisticated long-range missiles and also weapons of mass destruction. The Iraqi regime, courting Arab approval, made no secret of its ambitions to produce advanced weapon systems, saying they were necessary to combat the threat from Israel.

This policy was indeed widely supported throughout the region because of popular resentment against perceived Western, especially American, double standards: pressurizing Iraq, an important Arab country, to desist from enhancing its military capability whilst saying nothing about Israel, a country well known to be in possession of nuclear weapons. Even Syria, Iraq's arch rival, publicly supported Iraq's right to defend itself against an Israeli nuclear threat.

Increasingly, throughout the early months of 1990, Iraqi rhetoric had another target: its neighbour Kuwait. Relations had deteriorated since the end of the Iraq–Iran war. Even during the conflict Iraq had been angered by the refusal of its Kuwaiti ally to lease, or otherwise hand over, the two strategic islands of Warba and Bubiyan at the mouth of the Shatt al-Arab waterway which would have been of considerable military value against Iran. Iraq also demanded a renegotiation of the border with the Emirate, claiming that besides the erection of military installations on Iraqi territory Kuwait was illegally exploiting the Rumeila oil field (partially straddled by the international frontier) – which, in its view, rightly belonged to Baghdad – and had 'stolen' $2.4 billion worth of Iraqi oil. The most serious charge was that both Kuwait and the United Arab Emirates (UAE) were overproducing oil well beyond the quotas laid down by OPEC, and had done so since 1981, thus drastically and deliberately reducing Iraq's income. This was perceived in Baghdad as another act of robbery by Kuwait and the UAE. Baghdad also indicated that the regime expected its Gulf war financial backers to release Iraq from its huge debts that had been incurred in defending them from Iranian aggression. In mid-July 1990, just prior to an important OPEC council meeting, Iraq warned that it might take military action against countries that continued to exceed oil quotas. Simultaneously two Iraqi divisions (30,000 troops) were moved up to the border with Kuwait.

Most analysts agree on Saddam Hussein's motives for this aggressive posture.[7] Apart from a bid to assume a leadership role, they were primarily economic. He desperately needed to increase his oil income, well nigh Iraq's sole source of quick money in what amounted to a 'one crop' economy, to finance his rearmament programme and to recoup the damage caused to the Iraqi economy by eight years of war. Certainly there was no way he could consider repaying the debts run up with Kuwait and his other Arab Gulf creditors. Strategic considerations also applied. One lesson learned from the war with Iran was that Iraq needed better territorial access to the Gulf to secure the sea approaches to the Shatt al-Arab. Readjustment of the border to include Warba and Bubiyan plus the added economic bonus of including the entire Rumeila oil field under Iraqi sovereignty was an attractive proposition. These were powerful motivations, but were they worth going to war over?

It seems unlikely that we will ever know for certain precisely when and exactly why Saddam decided to launch his invasion of Kuwait. Undoubtedly he was angered by Kuwait's stubborn refusal to bow to Iraqi pressure. The Emirate insisted on repayment of Iraq's Gulf war debt as a precondition to discussing the border. It had announced plans for the development of Bubiyan. It continued to overproduce beyond the OPEC quota, only agreeing to toe the line at the OPEC meeting of July. And it was publicly robust in countering the Iraqi propaganda campaign. To some analysts the extent of Kuwait robustness was surprising. Did the Amir have secret assurances of American military support? To others Kuwaiti 'intransigence' – the refusal to concede an inch to Iraq's demands despite the increasingly urgent attempts by mediators to reach a compromise – served only to humiliate Saddam and to provoke him into intemperate action.[8]

In the absence of authoritative primary source Iraqi material, uncertainty will continue to surround Saddam's decision to order his forces into Kuwait. Was it long premeditated or was it an act of sudden impetuosity? Against the background of increasing Iraqi military build up on the border with Kuwait there had been an apparently successful OPEC summit on 25 July (which raised the price of oil as demanded by Iraq). Nevertheless the Iraqi tanks started to roll within 12 hours following an inconclusive meeting chaired by King Fahd of Saudi Arabia on 1 August between the Kuwaiti Crown Prince and the Deputy Chairman of Iraq's Revolutionary Command Council (RCC).[9] But one thing does seem probable. Surely Saddam, impetuous or not, would not have attacked unless he believed he was going to get away with it.

It is on this point that conspiracy theories abound. Analysts have made much of a meeting between Saddam and the US Ambassador to Iraq, April Glaspie, on 25 July. Did she or did she not give a virtual green light to Saddam to pursue his quarrel with Kuwait without fear of US intervention?[10] She evidently believed from Saddam's reaction, which she reported to Washington, that there was no immediate danger of military action, as she promptly departed Iraq on leave.[11] Our view is that Saddam completely miscalculated the likely Western and indeed Arab governments' response to his act of aggression, believing that no one would reckon that Kuwait was worth a fight. Or if they did, they would hesitate to take on the might of the Iraqi armed forces, said to be the world's fourth largest with more than a million men under arms. He may well have intended to teach the Kuwaitis a lesson and withdraw his forces after achieving a readjustment of the disputed frontier in Iraq's favour, following the installation of a puppet government and the writing off of his debt. Subsequent manoeuvres seem to indicate that this was his intention, frustrated by developments that Saddam had simply failed to anticipate.

Space does not permit a blow-by-blow chronological account of events following the Iraqi seizure of Kuwait on 2 August 1990 up to its liberation as a result of Operation Desert Storm on 28 February 1991. There are, however, features worth highlighting – notably the unprecedented nature of the international response to Saddam's aggression. It came as no surprise that Washington reacted swiftly and angrily. Iraq possessed the second largest oil reserves in the world (perhaps 10 per cent of the total), a position significantly enhanced by its seizure of Kuwait (nearly another 10 per cent) and its prolific oil fields. The United States relied on imports for about 50 per cent of its oil requirements and it was not acceptable for it to be potentially held to ransom by a maverick autocrat like the Iraqi leader.

Moreover, it seemed possible in early August that Saddam, with his forces poised on the southern Kuwaiti border, was contemplating adding the even larger oil fields of Saudi Arabia to his conquests. American allies in the West were also highly alarmed and needed little persuasion to join forces with Washington in confronting the Iraqi regime – initially via the UN Security Council and subsequently in the Desert Shield/Desert Storm military coalition.

It was the Arab reaction to the attack by an Arab on a brother that dramatically changed the traditional pattern of regional alliances. For the first time since the creation of the Arab League, conservative regimes such as the Gulf monarchies made common cause with radical states like Syria and Libya.[12] Normally conservative monarchist Jordan, influenced by enthusiastic popular support for Saddam, refused to join in the condemnation of Iraq and opposed US and other Western involvement, calling for an 'Arab solution' to the crisis; in the circumstances of total disarray in the Arab world, oxymoronic to say the least. Two emergency meetings of the Arab League illustrated this lack of common purpose. The first, on the day after the invasion, had six out of the twenty-one members voting against the resolution to condemn the Iraqi invasion and insist on its unconditional withdrawal (Jordan, Mauritania, Sudan, Yemen, the PLO and Iraq itself), while Libya refused to endorse the resolution. At the second summit meeting on 10 August, twelve of the participants voted to send a deterrent force to Saudi Arabia to support the build up of primarily American troops preparing to defend the kingdom against possible Iraqi attack. On this occasion Libya declined to send soldiers, though still calling upon Saddam to withdraw his forces.

Official hostility to Iraq, as reflected by the actions of a majority of Arab governments, was not an accurate reflection of popular sentiment in many of these states. Two factors influenced the public mood. First, a widespread lack of genuine sympathy with Kuwait. The Emirate was widely disliked for its perceived arrogance, its unconvincing pretensions to non-alignment and patronizing use of its great oil wealth. Its treatment of resident guest workers and the large Palestinian community as third-class citizens also raised hackles. Kuwait's refusal to show any flexibility in its dispute with Iraq engendered a widespread feeling that it had done much needlessly to provoke Baghdad. Second, Saddam, despite his surprise at the robustness of the international response, demonstrated considerable skill in manipulating Arab street opinion in his support.

Saddam originally claimed he had sent forces into Kuwait in response to an appeal by patriotic insurgents who had overthrown the 'corrupt' Sabah regime. Having failed to establish a client regime consisting of credible Kuwaitis he proceeded to Plan B. He then announced that Kuwait had been 'reunited' with its motherland Iraq; in other words, annexed to become Baghdad's Nineteenth Province. Iraq had thus reclaimed its rightful birthright, and one of the artificial borders created by colonialists had been liquidated in the interests of Pan Arab unity.[13] He also sought to attract regional support by creating major linkage between his Kuwait operation and the wider Middle East dispute. In effect he proposed an Iraqi withdrawal from Kuwait in exchange for, at the very least, an international conference on Palestine. However, this proposal was rejected out of hand by the United States and its Western allies, who wanted nothing to do with any idea that might be seen to reward Iraqi aggression and enhance its standing in the region. It struck a populist chord, however, especially in Jordan, the West Bank and Gaza and the Maghreb States. As the crisis developed, the Iraqi leader continued to play to a popular gallery by posing as the new Arab champion prepared to stand up to Western bullies, the traditional supporters of Israel, against overwhelming odds. Subsequent 'Scud' missile attacks on Israel after the outbreak of war immensely enhanced his standing in much of the Arab street. He also sought through his rhetoric to add an Islamic dimension to the conflict, invoking an image of a new Saladin fighting a jihad (holy war) against the Crusader West. As part of this campaign he added the phrase Allah Akbar (God is Great) to the Iraqi flag. Given the perceived overwhelmingly secular nature of the Iraqi establishment, this was probably the least successful of his ploys.

But, despite his manoeuvring, Saddam made little impression on the wider international community. The UN Security Council quickly established the most comprehensive regime of sanctions ever imposed on a member state, passing a whole raft of unopposed resolutions. Iraq's invasion of Kuwait served as a catalyst to draw the former American and Soviet rivals together, and there was no clearer indication that some kind of 'new world order' had been created than the disappearance of references to 'East' and 'West' from the discussion of international crisis management. However, such harmony was more of an indication that the Soviet star was on the wane and more preoccupied with domestic issues than any real meeting of minds in Washington and Moscow.

Although the international community, including the Security Council, called for a peaceful outcome to the crisis, seeking unconditional Iraqi withdrawal, the build up to military confrontation was inevitable. By the beginning of 1991 700,000 Desert Shield coalition forces had assembled – mostly in Saudi Arabia – outnumbering the half a million Iraqi troops thought by then to be in Kuwait. A multi-national armada of 200 naval ships had also been sent to the Gulf. Reports of Iraqi brutality in Kuwait, Saddam's abuse of civilian hostages trapped in the country and plans to use them as potential 'human shields' to deter military attack, plus his refusal, despite many attempts at mediation, to withdraw from the Emirate on acceptable terms hardened international opinion against him. Moreover, the US leadership stepped up the pressure for military action, fearing that a long stalemate that sanctions seemed unlikely to end would erode public support for armed conflict. The legal basis for going to war was provided by Security Council Resolution (SCR) 678 of 29 November 1990 which authorized 'all necessary means' to liberate Kuwait. Last-minute mediation attempts, notably by the Soviet Union, failed to prevent the outbreak of hostilities, code named 'Operation Desert Storm', on 16 and 17 January 1991.

The war was nasty, brutal and short. The forty-day air campaign consisting of over 90,000 missions wreaked havoc on Iraq's military and industrial infrastructure. Iraq's only effective counter – the use of the Scud missile – was nearly successful in widening the war by involving Israel, which was restrained by massive US military assistance from direct retaliation, which would have threatened the cohesion of an Arab–Western alliance. This mainly one-sided aerial assault, with more bombs dropped than during the Second World War, was followed by the 100-hour rout of the land campaign, which led to the liberation of Kuwait. This campaign inflicted heavy casualties on the fleeing Iraqi contingents of what proved to be a paper tiger of a military machine quite incapable of fighting the 'Mother of all Battles' proclaimed by the Iraqi leader.[14]

Saddam had not committed the 'crack' Republican Guard to the defence of Kuwait (nor did he deploy biological or chemical weapons) – wisely, as it transpired, as the Republican Guard was needed to crush revolts in the predominantly Shi'a southern Iraq and by the Kurds in the north. The US-led coalition was criticized in some quarters for neither pressing on to Baghdad to remove Saddam nor assisting the rebellions. But the first was not within the mandate of SCR 678 and the US, with memories of Vietnam, was reluctant (in both cases) to be involved in what could become a long-term messy campaign. This despite the US President's apparent encouragement of the uprisings when he addressed the Iraqi people following the ceasefire,[15] although it seems unlikely that either the Shi'ites or the Kurds needed much prompting to take advantage of what must have seemed a good opportunity to assert themselves. Moreover, Washington did not wish to see Iraq disintegrate. Eventually the Americans and British provided some protection for the Shi'ites and the Kurds via the establishment of 'no-fly zones' in the south and north of Iraq. They later created a safe haven for the Kurds, barring Iraqi aircraft from both sectors.

As we pointed out at the beginning of this chapter, ten years after Desert Storm little of real substance changed in the region. Above all the same divisions in the Arab world were still apparent; although, admittedly, the Jordanian and Palestinian leaderships have managed to mend most of the fences damaged by their stance during the crisis. The Jordanians have also successfully absorbed 300,000 Palestinian–Jordanian refugees expelled or refused permission to return to Kuwait where they were long-term residents. But there had been no Arab or indeed wider international consensus of how to deal with Iraq. Popular attitudes and the views of elites and regimes remained far apart. A decade of draconian sanctions linked to the dismantlement of Iraq's arms industry damaged, but probably did not destroy Saddam's capacity to produce weapons of mass destruction. At the turn of the century he remained entrenched in power with little apparent prospect of departure. Sanctions were widely perceived to have been more damaging to his people than influential with the regime and attracted widespread public sympathy, in the West as well as in the Arab world, for the ordinary Iraqi who failed to benefit from the humanitarian provisions of the sanctions legislation. The UN, including governments previously supportive of the coalition, were increasingly divided over confronting and punishing Iraq, and especially on the issue of how to enforce the arms inspection and monitoring regime. Two intensive (Anglo-American) air campaigns since 1991 to enforce Iraqi co-operation with the UN failed to achieve their objectives. Subsequent aggressive enforcement of the no-fly zones by US and British warplanes attracted widespread international criticism.

Hopes in the West that one outcome of the defeat of Iraq on behalf of the Gulf monarchies would lead to more democratization in the region have largely been disappointed. At the time of the war, US and other Western commentators had expressed unease about going to war on behalf of monarchical regimes seemingly almost as autocratic as their Iraqi enemy. Although the National Assembly was restored in Kuwait its narrow franchise remained unchanged. There has been timid liberalization in Qatar and Oman (although more so in Bahrain), but Saudi Arabia and the UAE remain montholithically undemocratic. Progress towards significant constitutional liberalization in Jordan predates the Gulf conflict, and continued popular support for Iraq (if not now for its leader) had been a factor in renewed authoritarianism by the late King Hussein and his successor. One positive outcome, however, has been the re-launch of the Middle East Peace Process. But this more reflects the unchallenged predominance of the US as the main external player in the region, and Palestinian impotence, than any recognition of the validity of Saddam's 'linkage' between the Gulf and developments in the Levant.[16] As Cordesman (1996) argued, in the wake of the coalition's victory, 'Like it or not, the US is the only nation that can assemble and project enough power to meet any aggressor. While Americans may not want to be the world's policeman, they must consider what it could be like to live in a world without any policeman at all.'

Indeed, whether or not it has the role of 'the world's policeman', it is the very visible dominance of the United States that is the most striking legacy of the part that Washington played in orchestrating and prosecuting Desert Storm at the beginning of the 1990s. Without continual US pressure it is likely that regional countries, with the exception of Kuwait and Saudi Arabia, would have made their peace with Iraq by the turn of the century. US insistence had held the sanctions regime together, ragged at the edges though it had become. North American commercial interests riding on the back of US military and political influence had substantially increased their share of an already lucrative market. Washington never ceased to remind its friends and allies in the Arab Gulf that its ready help at times of trouble merited commercial recompense, whether through yet more purchases of military hardware or by the award of very large civil contracts to US companies.

Nor was Washington reluctant to remind the Gulf monarchies of its role as protector of last resort in the face of the threat that Saddam Hussein was still believed to present to the region despite his crushing defeat. Sanctions might help to keep Saddam in his cage but only the US had the muscle to put him back behind bars whenever he might try to break out. So, to a great extent, as some cynics have argued, it suited the US to have the neighbourhood bully still at large, thus justifying its position as the policeman on the block. By the end of the twentieth century, Saddam had shown no signs of an early departure from a scene he had dominated so long. However, the start of the new millennium and the arrival of a new US administration, headed by the veterans of this Gulf war encounter, appears to have initiated, after the dramatic events of 9/11, a countdown towards the inevitable conflict we describe in our final chapter. Even without the events of 9/11 many believed that it was only a matter of time before the administration of George W. Bush finished business with Iraq that had been initiated by his father a decade earlier.

9   The politics of conflict and failure of peacemaking

It is a safe prediction that conflict in the Middle East will never be fully resolved, nor for that matter will it be fully resolved anywhere else. Nevertheless, levels of conflict and how they interrelate can be reduced or controlled, and in some cases removed. However, the most important point to be made about conflict and peacemaking since 1945 in the Middle East is that it was not until the early 1990s that substantial progress towards the formal conclusion of peace treaties was achieved within the region.

Conflict resolution as a meaningful process has taken the best part of fifty years to emerge as a process in which parties to conflict can effectively engage in. This is not to ignore Kissinger's shuttle diplomacy of the 1970s or the Egyptian–Israeli Peace Treaty of the same era, nor the numerous plans and proposals outlined by successive US administrations since their increasing involvement in the region following the decline of Britain and France after the Second World War. Rather, it is to put such efforts into historical context, a context that actually mitigated against any serious attempt to address the real issues at the heart of so many conflicts in the region. Indeed, we believe that in many respects it was only with the ending of the cold war and superpower competition in the Middle East that progress has been made in the major arena of conflict in the region, the Arab–Israeli and Palestinian–Israeli conflict. We would caution, however, that without a more comprehensive approach to conflict resolution and appropriate linkages to other political and economic issues in the region, there is still a serious likelihood that conflicts such as those in Iraq could undermine the wider goals of peacemakers. Such an approach, however, also requires a major adjustment of the current Western mindset towards the region's majority Muslim population, which is currently perceived as part of one suppurating mass of Islamic violence, repression and primitivism that threatens Western interests in the region.

In September 1993 when Israeli Prime Minister Yitzhak Rabin and PLO President Yasser Arafat shook hands on the lawn of the White House at the conclusion of the Declaration of Principles, the rest of the world declared that peace had at last been achieved in the Middle East. The white dove with its olive branch had finally shown up in the region where conflict had become a way of life for citizens and of politics between states. Many may have rubbed their eyes in wonderment at two battle-hardened combatants finally, if grudgingly, grasping the prize of peace. Indeed, both Rabin and Arafat were formerly regarded as men of war, each with battle experience under their belts, each the declared enemy of the other. Now heralded as a 'peace of the brave', the ability of military men to put the past behind them and grasp the hand of friendship was promoted by pundits and commentators alike as a symbol of how far along the path to peace the leaders of the Israelis and Palestinians had come. Such figures added a legitimacy to a difficult and hard process of peacemaking.

But on the same day away from the White House in Washington and within the Middle East itself a different picture emerged. There was very little celebration, an absence of euphoria, no dancing in the streets, no victory parades and parties, no national days of rejoicing. Instead there was a recognition that the first, not last, difficult step on a long road had been undertaken by participants who were largely cajoled and pressurized into peacemaking by outside players and major powers. For many the picture of the famous Rabin–Arafat handshake was too much to take in. Generations within the region had battled with each other, subsisting on national images demonizing the enemy with atavistic abhorrence. Yet now the 'peace of the brave' was declared from on high. Peacemaking became a daunting novel prospect and the familiar certainties of conflict remained all too alluring for their leaders whose authority and survival in the region depended on the military.

To argue that many in the Middle East might have a stronger stake in conflict than in peace and stability might sound perverse. The fact is, however, that many of the region's political systems have been dominated for many decades by antagonisms around which political power, economic decisions and regional alliances have been constructed. The political and economic elite of many states within the region have prospered on conflict and its associated commerce in arms. Internal political divisions and discontents have often been suppressed through appeals to national unity in the face of the enemy from outside not within. The prevalence of the military in the political systems of the region, as we discussed in the introduction to this book, is immense even in democracies like Israel where, as Arian has remarked, 'the boundaries between the civilian and the military . . . are not clear . . . With the army being so esteemed, so prominent, and so important, it is not surprising that it is also so powerful.'[1] Associated arms spending in the region is prolific and higher than any other developing area of the world, and with little evidence of decline to date.

Thus, those who may be said to have a stake in conflict are admittedly few in number, but enough of them form the core elite in many states in the region to make their perspective matter. These political leaders are rhetorically bound into the cycle of what appears to be interminable conflict; this is an image they project at national as well as regional and even global level. Breaking out of such habit-forming behaviour appears almost impossible. In striking the pose of conflict it is no wonder that so many have viewed the Middle East through the kaleidoscope of war, conflict, bloodshed, soldiers, terrorism and guns, and why so many have talked about the region in terms of a cycle of war, conflagration and antagonism.

Yet, as the region stood on the threshold of a new century, signs of major conflict or full-scale war had been absent for a decade. Lebanon, Israel–Palestine, Israeli–Arab, Iran–Iraq, Kuwait and Yemen could all be cited as territories, arenas where major conflict and war had subsided or dissolved into complex political emergencies.[2] Indeed, the closing decades and particularly the events of the last decade of the twentieth century contributed to what might be called new patterns of conflict transformation and peacebuilding. If major conflict such as war is currently in abeyance, however, it is not an indicator that peace and stability have increased in prominence. Major conflict has been replaced by minor conflicts or complex political emergencies that more often than not reflect internal rather than inter-state disputes.

The regional arms race, particularly the nuclear capacity of at least Israel and possibly Iran, has also played its part as a preventive strategy for ruling out the kind of major wars that characterized the region for so many decades. Nuclear deterrence has its unwelcome place in the new regional balance of power where national indebtedness in terms of military spending is commonplace. The futility of developing economies dedicated to arms spending, arms production and arms procurement is barely recognized among the elites of Arab capitals across the region and beyond. The race to acquire or develop more and more sophisticated weaponry systems, and the willingness of Western governments and others to supply arms, continues apace.

Since 1945 attempts at peacemaking within the region have been perceived as largely unsuccessful. Indeed the response to conflict seemed to be an extra effort in exacerbating conditions rather than seeking the peaceful resolution of the major conflicts that had brought so many states within the region to the battlefield. For many years the most that was hoped for in the field of peacemaking was internationally mediated ceasefire agreements. In addition the politics of peacemaking was not deemed positive enough in the national and regional arenas from which political leaders took their cue.

Political legitimacy was all too often tied to aggression, belligerence and a vocabulary of conflict. The nature of leadership within the region was, for so many decades, predicated on the notion of strength through aggression and conflict. President Gamal Abdel Nasser of Egypt, probably the greatest Arab leader of the twentieth century, underpinned his leadership of Egypt and his bid for the regional crown by prompting an agenda of belligerence, in particular against Israel but also in relations with Jordan, Iraq and Syria, and on the side of one of the parties in the civil conflict in Yemen in the late 1960s. His very roots lay in the Egyptian military, and the *coup d'état* launched by the Egyptian Free Officers in 1952 and the establishment of the Egyptian republic was but one episode in a phenomenon that characterized the region throughout the 1950s and 1960s.

Israel is another example where the military and conflict mentality has dominated the conduct of diplomacy and regional relations for decades. Even when Israel has succeeded in concluding peace with its closest neighbours, the peace that is forged is largely diplomatic and has not extended to the citizens of either party to peace. Thus, it would not be unfair to assert that mutual loathing and animosity has been the key characteristic behind so many supposedly key relationships within the region, whether between Israel and Lebanon, Syria and Iraq, Iraq and Iran, Egypt and Libya, Syria and Jordan, Iran and Israel, Saudi Arabia and Egypt, and so on. Does all of this mean that peacemaking is doomed to perpetual failure in the region?

In short, no. Although with the new millennium witnesssing the almost complete collapse of the MEPP, plus the recent invasion of Iraq, it is tempting to be more pessimistic. Nevertheless, peacemaking has developed in a variety of ways. Major political changes in the late 1980s occurred regionally and globally to create a new platform from which peacemaking could be launched. Peacemaking, or perhaps more appropriately conflict trans-formation, has finally, albeit with great difficulty in some quarters, entered the vocabulary of policy-makers and political leaders across the region.[3] The futility of conflict has sometimes been recognized independently but mostly through the role, coercive or otherwise, of external actors or mediators. Indeed it would be foolhardy in the extreme to ignore the impact that external third parties and the internationalization of conflict have had on attempts at conflict resolution in the Middle East. It would, for example, be impossible to understand the dynamics of the Middle East peace process in the 1990s without factoring-in the role of the US and its position as a hegemonic global superpower. In addition, the question of the impact that the United Nations has had on resolving the conflict, rather than just condemning actors through Security Council resolutions, needs to be acknowledged. Finally, the growing or potential import of transnational bodies such as the European Union must be acknowledged when examining the thorny issue of external involvement in conflict transformation in the region. Indeed, Rupesinghe has argued that 'the chances of successfully resolving a dispute are much higher if national and international agencies and organisations can be persuaded to combine their efforts'.[4]

Many factors, however, need to be critically assessed to determine the required minimum to maintain the momentum for peace in the region. Such factors include the changing pattern of global politics and the end to superpower rivalry in the Middle East, economic issues linked to globalization and the region's poor performance in global markets, the impact of oil prices on world markets, and the religious dimension of some conflicts in the region which concern millions of adherents to one faith or the other across the globe. This issue in particular was brought into sharp relief during the Palestinian–Israeli negotiations on Jerusalem in summer 2000 and the subsequent crisis of violence and conflict in the autumn of that year. The issue of Jerusalem ignited violence not only between Israelis and Palestinians in the Holy Land, but in New York, London, south Asia, Yemen and elsewhere. Violent protest, conflict and mutual antagonism underscored the import of this issue to Muslims and Jews across the world.

Conflict resolution, the methods by which wars and other conflicts are ended and resolved, has also changed. Traditional methods and roles remain in some contexts, but in others they have been diminished by new ways of making peace, which include indigenous and regional-based solutions. Indeed, there is evidence of an increasing resistance in many quarters to external mediation of processes of conflict resolution in the region and an increasing reliance on local traditional methods of dispute resolution which are more inclusive of religious elements, tribal leaders or other elements in society.

The types of conflict resolution and successes associated with them have also varied considerably. Major long-term conflicts have been resolved through peace treaties brokered by international actors, predominantly the USA. Civil conflict in Lebanon has been resolved as a result of regional actors bringing the warring parties to the negotiating table. The UN has been responsible for helping to forge peace between Iran and Iraq, and European efforts have been conspicuous in attempts to resolve the Algerian conflict. Yet what accounts for the renewed interest in peacemaking and conflict resolution within the region? Before this question is answered it is important to make some distinctions. Peace-building, peacemaking, peace processes, conflict resolution and conflict transformation are all separate but related activities. Peace is not something that can be achieved overnight in the Middle East. Nor should the formal cessation of hostilities in the form of signed agreements be viewed as an end to conflict. It is not even enough to presuppose that the conclusion of peace treaties between states means that peace has truly been achieved between the citizens of those states. Unfortunately 'cold peace' is a term all too familiar a concept in the region.

The first seismic shift in global politics to impact on the prospects for peacemaking in the Middle East was the end of the cold war and the collapse of the Soviet Union in 1989. While the immediate results of this were clearly discernible in the Gulf crisis and the decline of Soviet support for radical Arab states such as Syria, the impact on the politics of peacemaking were not so easily discernible. In many respects the change can only be ascertained by a retrospective focus. For example, the nature of peacemaking between Israel and Egypt in the late 1970s, following the war of 1973, was utterly altered by superpower rivalry in the region and the battle for hegemony between the United States and the Soviet Union. The *détente* relationship had been severely tested in this theatre of the cold war and extended to peacemaking brokered by these superpowers. With the absence of the Soviet Union would the US play a different role within the region when it came to the realm of peace politics?

The change in the balance of power and an increasing perception of US hegemony in the region led many to believe that US national interest – as represented through foreign policy – would shape the future of the Middle East, with capitulation the order of the day in a series of Arab capitals that had traditionally been hostile to the USA. It was expected that Syria, for example, bereft of its Soviet patron, would be propelled into the arms of the American State Department. In reality Washington has discovered that there is a limit to its influence in the region, particularly in pushing traditional enemies together and bringing them together to negotiate peace. The first round of multi-lateral peace conferences in 1991, which brought Syrian and Israeli negotiators together for the first time, was misleading because the Syrian President Hafez al-Assad would only travel so far along the road to peace. In addition, the State Department in Washington faced a hostile Congress that maintained that Syria was a 'terrorist state' to which no concessions, even in the name of peace, could be countenanced. Similar accusations are now being made again in the wake of regime change in Baghdad with members of the US 'hard right' implying that the Syrian regime is next in line. America's traditional allies, however, have continued to benefit from a 'special relationship' which is able to withstand the pulls and pushes of everyday politics in the region. Yet, as Halliday reminds us, 'To ascribe all of the region's ills to Washington's actions or inaction, is facile. To argue consistently that alternative possibilities are preferable and practicable is not.'[5] Evidence of consideration of these new approaches are to be found not only in those spheres of the American orbit in the Middle East such as the Palestinian–Israeli peace process, but also in those orbits where other actors have a greater interest or influence, such as the Lebanese peace process where Arab and European actors have played a greater role.

Out of a changing political climate, with America achieving a greater profile in the Middle East yet also determined to ensure that European and other actors play a role where necessary, the new economic landscape has yet to be evaluated. Making war is an expensive business and turning guns into ploughshares has the potential radically to alter and improve living standards in a number of states across the region. In addition, there is a prevalent belief in aid, development and diplomatic circles that with peace a new stability will be generated across the region that will promote greater economic unity and suitable economies of scale, and decrease dependency and indebtedness. Thus, not only will peace mean that the governments of the region devote less of their resources to the military and more to welfare and education, but that improved diplomatic relations will promote inter-regional trade agreements that will assist liberalizing economies. In Israel, for example, if peace agreements are reached with Syria, the Palestinians and Lebanon, not only will the government have to devote less to its standing army and arms industry but the potential markets of the Arab world will be realized for Israeli goods, particularly those in the technology sector.

Another indication that economics matters is the willingness of the international community to promote peace and sponsor peace processes and confidence-building measures through aid and loans. In the late 1980s, and again in the early 1990s, King Hussein of Jordan faced mounting economic pressures in his own country that had already sparked off public unrest and riots. But with the underpinning of his peace deal with Israel by American aid, and loans from the World Bank and the International Monetary Fund (IMF), risking the wrath of his vehemently anti-Israeli citizenry became a realistic proposition. Nor can there be any doubt that without the promise of a peace dividend within the American-sponsored orbit, Jordan would not have climbed aboard the peace train that culminated in a treaty with Israel in November 1994. Yet while many believed that Israel would deliver the bulk of the economic dividend, the reality was that the international community – through bilateral and multi-lateral assistance, loans and direct aid – would shore up the economy and aid it to withstand popular discontent at the King's political gamble. The same is true in Lebanon, where, following the end of Israel's occupation of the south in May 2000, the international community reiterated its commitment to assist the process of peace and reconstruction through aid and loans. On the other hand, since 1990 Iraq's population suffered under the regime of internationally imposed sanctions as a result of the conflict with Kuwait. If the UN-imposed sanctions were designed to bring the regime of Saddam Hussein to its knees and prevent further military escapades then they failed; instead they had the effect, thanks to cynical manipulation by the Iraqi regime, only in raising rates of infant mortality, disease and malnutrition and penalizing the most vulnerable and helpless sectors of Iraqi society. The resumption of the weapons inspection programme, the rupture of international opinion, a crisis wrought on the head of the United Nations, and a further pre-emptive military action in which hundreds of thousands of American and other allied troops were amassed in the Gulf in early 2003 was the way in which certain quarters of the international community sought to achieve the kind of regime change that did not take place in 1991. Along the way the legitimacy of war was severely scrutinized and immense disquiet was palpable in the majority of Arab capitals. In Middle East peacemaking talks, economic considerations loom like a spectre at the feast at the negotiating tables.

Economic issues, therefore, even in the wealthier states of the Gulf, have compelled policy-makers and political leaders to consider new ways of conducting inter-state relations and regional competitions for leadership. Even Saudi Arabia and Kuwait, two of the wealthiest states in the world, were forced to rethink peace strategies in the wake of the 1990 debacle with Iraq. With a decline in oil prices, growing dependency on imports and expanding populations, the leaders of these states were compelled to assess the cost of conflict, and this was largely reflected in national plans that emerged in the latter part of the 1990s.

In the wake of the Gulf crisis, with the collapse of old Arab–Arab and Arab–Iranian relationships and the decline in the importance of maverick leaders like Hafez al-Assad and Muammar Ghadaffi, some new patterns formerly associated with the politics of conflict have emerged. Such patterns are nascent and it would be premature, for example, to declare that a new era of Arab unity mirroring that of the 1960s or 1970s can be discerned. This also presupposes that such unity was ever achieved in reality any-way. Nevertheless, the rhetoric and postures of hostility, mutual suspicion and antagonism that characterized so many regional relationships within the Arab orbit, as well as in the Arab–Israeli, Iranian–Israeli or Iranian–Arab spheres, show signs of decline or change. So much sabre rattling in the name of Arab unity has been replaced by new statements about unity through partnership and peace. War-weary Iranians, Syrians, Saudis, Lebanese, Iraqis, Kurds, Shi'a and Islamists have developed novel strategies for achieving their goals which increasingly involve negotiation, compromise, peace-building and power-sharing. The importance of such initiatives lies not in their achievements but in the new dialogues emerging in some Arab circles.

The role of the Arab League in brokering an end to the civil war in Lebanon in 1990 highlights new approaches. The Taif Accord, which signalled an end to conflict in Lebanon, was negotiated by three Arab actors: the Arab League, the governments of Saudi Arabia and Syria and a tripartite commission of the Kings of Morocco and Saudi Arabia and President Chadli Benjedid of Algeria. In this context the tireless efforts of Arab diplomats and political leaders in both the regional structure of the Arab League and the individual mediator states resulted in an end to what was generally considered to be intractable conflict that had destroyed the very fabric of Lebanon over a fifteen-year period. The success of such efforts, however, are only explicable in the context of the new global balance of power and the willingness of the US to allow the Arabs to negotiate their own way out of this particular conflict.[6]

Negotiation, stalled, erratic, fuelled by emotion and political rhetoric, has become a new political game in the conduct of conflict transformation at an inter-state level in the region. Negotiation processes, however, can take many forms, including pre-negotiation negotiations, bilateral or multi-lateral talks, first, second and third track negotiations, as well as issue-specific negotiations. Formal and informal dialogue and processes had characterized relations within the region, particularly around the issue of the Arab–Israeli conflict and associated off-shoot conflicts throughout the 1990s. Approaches to negotiating processes, therefore, need to be understood and contextualized in terms of the rules of this game.

While negotiation was perceived as a form of externally imposed capitulation, weakness from within, and an acknowledgement that the conflict could not be won by other means, it had little value in the Middle Eastern context. For, after all, these conflicts allowed people to live insular community-based lives eschewing major episodes of contact with the other as an acknowledgement of their existence; a mindset that allowed no room for the enemy. The recognition that negotiation entailed dialogue as well as acceptance or recognition of the enemy was an important feature in conflict transformation in the Arab–Israeli and Palestinian–Israeli conflict throughout the 1990s. In addition, trust-building as both a prerequisite and a primary feature of such processes had been essential, yet at the same time most difficult to achieve. The difficulties were encountered within the first months of the twenty-first century and ruptured by the events that followed the outbreak of the second Palestinian uprising in September 2000. Those involved in the Oslo process failed to surmount the final obstacles and garner support for trust and concession as frantic final status talks were convened by the Clinton administration.

Negotiation, then, became meaningful only when recognition, trust-building, compromise and compensation entered the vocabulary of the peacemakers. Problem-sharing is the key to problem-solving; as Flamhaft illustrates in the Israeli–Palestinian context, three factors determine the point at which the time is ripe to negotiate: 'the combatants' conclusion that the continuation of the status quo would only worsen their situation, their simultaneous desire to reach an agreement . . . [and] the domestic support for a negotiated solution'.[7]

The Oslo process, which followed the very public failure of the Madrid Conferences (1991–1993), was shrouded in secrecy and involved, for the first time, direct recognition of the PLO and contact between the Israeli government and PLO officials. The failure of Madrid, where Shamir had refused to recognize the PLO as the legitimate representatives of the Palestinian people and had engaged in a public strategy of stalling and intransigence, had only served to reinforce mutual suspicion and mistrust. Secrecy, on the other hand, was the key to the success of the Oslo talks; negotiators were free from external pressures and interference – exactly the type of interference that had characterized the American and Russian-sponsored Madrid process. The bedrock of the Oslo process, however, was recognition and trust-building. On the Israeli side indirect recognition occurred in two ways. First, the secret talks were to be held directly with a member of the PLO and not through a delegated conduit such as the Jordanians. Second, in January 1993 Israeli law repealed the ban on contacts with the PLO. As Abu Odeh highlights, 'Rabin was the first Israeli leader to recognize the Palestinians as a peace partner to be approached rather than as an obstacle to be by-passed. The DOP attests to that.'[8] The ground rules outlined at the first meetings in January 1993 reveal much about the processes of pre-negotiation and negotiation. The two sides agreed that there would be 'no dwelling on past grievances, total secrecy, and retractibility of all positions put forward in the talks'; from this point constructive dialogue and then negotiation could take place.[9]

Secrecy, trust-building and recognition, however, cannot guarantee any peace process and the stalled timetabling of such processes illustrates the impact that time and motion can have on the so-called momentum for peace. The achievement of peace treaties, agreements and timetables for future negotiation and resolution of outstanding issues is admirable, but remains conspicuous by its absence in the context of the Middle East; these are national governmental and non-governmental strategies that engage citizens in inter-state peace-building measures. To date, much of the peace-making and confidence building that has occurred in the region has been limited to the elite. The prospects for a generational change in attitudes towards the futility of major conflict, acts of political violence and harm to each other have not been achieved, despite the emergence of a dynamic motivated younger generation of citizens who are increasingly aware of their position, not just in the region but within the global system. For, as Halliday has suggested, 'relations between the states of the region themselves remain dominated by suspicion, conflict and latent (when not overt) confrontation'.[10] Certainly, externally imposed solutions to conflict in the region will ultimately fail to address core national interests and citizens' rights in a global era. Externally imposed solutions, while professing even-handedness, neutrality and mediation rather than intimidation, are nevertheless motivated by economic and strategic concerns about maintaining the global balance of power both politically and economically in the Western orbit. Wars to 'bring democracy' to the region fail to convince subject populations that the intentions of such liberators are as honourable as they claim to be. For this is the point in which the collective historical memory which is so important to so many in the region comes to the forefront. For the Iraqis, for instance when British Prime Minister Tony Blair declared that the war on Iraq in March 2003 was about liberating the Iraqi people and not conquering them, the bitter memory of Britain's own less-than-glorious meddling in Iraq was revived. For the same promises were uttered by the British General Maude during the First World War when he conquered Baghdad, promising the people: 'Our armies do not come into your cities and lands as conquerors or enemies, but as liberators . . . Your wealth has been stripped off you by unjust men . . . The people of Baghdad shall flourish . . . '[11] Less than five years later the British as one of the spoils of war had created Iraq as a mandate territory, a highly artifical construction subject to their authority and to that of a puppet monarch and not reflecting the aspirations of the local people. There is a residual fear in the region of history repeating itself – this time with America replacing Britain or France as the imperial power keen to secure its economic and strategic interests at the expense of the rights of the native people of the area. The tentative emergence of local methods of conflict dispute, such as religious- or tribal-based conciliation processes, does offer some hope that the region may emerge from its conflicts to establish new relationships of peace-building rather than slipping back into the atavistic grip of a Hobbesian state of war, which so many in the West have credited the region with in the past. To assume the former rather than the latter is to credit the citizens of the region with the same human values of compassion and peace as anywhere else in the world. Accepting the latter, however, might also imply that while so many states of the region remain dominated by authoritarian leaders and their military machines, the ordinary citizens will remain immobilized by oppression and conflict. Additionally, however, the prospect of liberation, by any means, does not necessarily promise automatic upgrading to freedom, equality and liberty. In the twenty-first century, as much as at any other time in the Middle East, one is reminded of the words of Agatha Christie, who remarked in a different context that one 'is left with a horrible feeling now that war settles nothing; that to win a war is as disastrous as to lose one'. The challenge is to exert as much effort and resources into peace-making in the region as has been devoted to militarization and conflict.

10 After the storm

And after these things I saw another angel come down from heaven, having great power; and the earth was lightened with his glory. And he cried mightily with a strong voice, saying, Babylon the great is fallen, is fallen, and is become the habitation of devils, and the hold of every foul spirit, and a cage of every unclean and hateful bird. For all nations have drunk of the wine of the wrath of her fornication, and the kings of the earth have committed fornication with her, and the merchants of the earth are waxed rich through the abundance of her delicacies.

Revelation XVIII, King James Bible

The day the world appeared to pause and understand the frailty of human life since 1945 was 11 September 2001 when members of an Islamist terror organization named al-Qaeda (the base) and led by Usama bin Laden launched a series of attacks on New York and Washington. Hundreds lost their lives on the planes that were hijacked and driven by the hijackers into buildings that symbolized American military, economic and political power. Thousands died as a result of the attack. The American people experienced a direct sense of terrifying vulnerability, but the shock waves were felt world-wide.

The instant judgement on the terrorist attacks was that 'it changed everything'.[1] The twentieth-century tradition of nation-states in conflict had been, at a stroke, transformed into the twenty-first century fear of a new world disorder, with the prospect of the 'evil' forces of fanatical transnational terrorism challenging the established basis of civilized society on an unprecedented scale. In this instance, the shadowy network of al-Qaeda, controlled by Usama bin Laden, was perceived as taking on 'the West', as represented by the United States of America. In this sense 'the West' was understood as representative of values that bin Laden contested. The locus of the new conflict, the seed-bed of Islamist hate, the region that spawned the callous suicide-bombers, was the Middle East.

The 'Middle Eastern and Islamist connection' to the attacks, assumed from the outset, resonated strongly throughout Western capitals such as Washington, London and Rome. In this respect the Middle East was once again perceived in many quarters as a harbinger of conflict, with Islamic dimensions to boot. This revived notions of a clash of civilizations, with Islam and the West facing each other across an ever-widening chasm. Under this notion the West led and Islam trailed in the wake of the progressive, democratic and plural values of the new world order shaped by non-Muslim power. Indeed, in the wake of the attacks Italian Prime Minister Berlusconi declared, 'We must be aware of the superiority of our civilization, a system that has guaranteed well-being, respect for human rights and – in contrast with Islamic countries – respect for religious and political rights.'[2]

The response from quarters of the international community made vulnerable by al-Qaeda's attacks was to declare a 'global war on terrorism' (GWOT). In an address to the American nation in the wake of the attacks US President George W. Bush outlined the portent of the conflict with terrorism, declaring that, 'This is not, however, just America's fight. And what is at stake is not just America's freedom. This is the world's fight. This is civilization's fight. This is the fight of all who believe in progress and pluralism, tolerance and freedom.' Thus the war on terrorism was declared and President Bush outlined in stark terms the American position to states in the international order, including those of the Middle East, 'You're either with us or against us in the fight against terror.' The mood in Washington, or more specifically the dominant elements of the Bush administration, now mattered more than ever in terms of the prospects for conflict and peacemaking in the Middle East. It has been noted that, 'Since the al-Qaeda attacks Americans have thought differently about their vulnerability, their power and the need to use that power in faraway places in order to feel safe at home. Because America has changed, the world has changed too.'[3] The greatest change, with major implications for the Middle East, was the feeling in Washington of confidence, almost triumphalism, springing from the success of the initial stages of the GWOT. The campaign against the Taliban government and al-Qaeda in Afghanistan was launched within three months of 9/11 and waged by a US-led coalition allied to anti-Taliban elements within Afghanistan itself.

Self-congratulation was not out of place. The rapid removal of the Taliban regime from Afghanistan, with negligible loss of Allied lives, was a remarkable achievement. It was achieved despite concern that the allied coalition could, like the Russians before them, be sucked into a long, bloody campaign with the odds stacked against them. With the ejection of the Taliban as the governing force and the installation of a new broad interim governing force (the Loya Jirga), the main task appeared to have been achieved in terms of Afghanistan being understood as the seat of terror in this region. Usama bin Laden also lost out on a wider front. Despite his appeals there were no uprisings against moderate Muslim regimes with close links to the West stigmatized as being part of a 'Zionist–Crusader alliance'. The jihad, as a form of conflict undertaken by ordinary Muslims in the Middle East, never materialized. The anti-Western demonstrations in a number of Muslim countries were less in both quantity and qualitative fervour than bin Laden must have hoped, but the fact that they took place at all contributed to a sense of disquiet and alarm in the United States of America. Countless Muslim leaders and preachers, as well as ordinary people, condemned bin Laden's act as terrorism not jihad and accused him of bringing the name of Islam into terrible disrepute. Even elements of radical Islamism distanced themselves from such deeds and refuted claims that their struggles, their resistance, even if undertaken by violent means, could be equated with the acts perpetrated by al-Qaeda on American targets.

As noted in Chapter 3, perceived success on the Afghan front encouraged elements of the Bush administration to widen the GWOT. 'Axis of Evil' references to Iraq, Iran and North Korea in Bush's State of the Union speech jarred on many ears in the Middle East and was widely ridiculed for its jingoistic 'OK Corral' presentation. But this was not just chest thumping. The jungle drums conveyed a serious message. The epithet: 'axis of evil', reminiscent of a previous President's memorable description of the former Soviet Union as an 'evil empire', together with deliberate leaks of a US Pentagon hit list of nuclear targets in a number of 'rogue' or potentially rogue states,[4] signalled Washington's resolve to deal severely with any government that it assumed presented a grave threat to its security. A risk to security was taken as meaning, among other things, unconcealed or clandestine support for movements such as al-Qaeda, or a whole host of other groups from the Middle East region designated as 'terrorist'. In this respect most states of the region, and a significant number of non-state actors, would fall under the scope of the US.

Indeed, by 2003 the FBI list of foreign organizations designated as terrorist by the USA had twenty-eight cited, of which eighteen originated or were based in the Middle East. Additionally, a threat to security was also defined by being in development or custody of weapons of mass destruction (WMD) which, because of the disposition of the regimes in question, could find their way into the hands of terrorists. There was a particular fear of an 'un-Holy' alliance between transnational terror elements such as al-Qaeda and the regime of Saddam Hussein in Iraq. In this case, and at that time, there was a lack of hard intelligence specifically linking the Iraq ruling clique and bin Laden and the ideological chasm between a religiously motivated extremist and a secular regime tended to be overlooked. However, as has been the case elsewhere amongst disparate radical groups, the one issue that was presumed to unite such unlikely bedfellows was anti-Americanism. Yet it was bin Laden's links with Saddam Hussein that President Bush had primarily in mind as he asserted on 11 March 2002: 'the war will not be over when the terrorist networks are disrupted, scattered and discredited but when the sources of the weapons of mass destruction they are seeking to obtain have been removed as well'. This pronouncement represented a new focus on the Middle East. Finding friendly governments in the region, which would be ready to prosecute the war on terrorism alongside the US, would be important. Yet, the prospect of an increased American presence in the Arab world, irrespective of the intent, alarmed many Arab leaders. Only the leadership in Israel seemed to find solace in the prospect that the US could take up arms in the region and prosecute military conflicts against some of its main enemies. Even on this front, however, there were tensions as the American administration urged restraint in relation to Mr Sharon and his attitude to the Palestinians, while they busily courted Arab support for an international coalition against the Taliban and al-Qaeda.

One of the more immediate manifestations of new conflicts in the Middle East – between an actor external to the region and state and non-state actors in the region – occurred in Yemen in the Arabian peninsula. There the US turned to the governing authorities and applied pressure to co-operate in the war against terrorism. Since late 2001 hundreds of US special forces have been stationed in Yemen (and neighbouring Djibouti) undertaking the training of Yemeni special forces, as well as manning their own missions against suspected Islamist elements. This has led to the government being targeted by anti-American and Islamist elements as 'stooges' of the USA and generated new tensions in an already fractious region. Yemeni political stability has never been taken for granted and, only a decade on from the reunification of the country, destabilization was an ever-present prospect. American involvement could create new problems in the not-too-distant future.

The US government was also anxious to build and maintain a long-term international alliance against terrorism. When the Taliban had been routed, the Iraqi President Saddam Hussein and his regime came into the frame as 'Public Enemy Number One' in the US hit list of 'rogue states'. President Clinton's policy of containment in respect of Iran and Iraq was now replaced with one of active and aggressive confrontation. With confrontation came consideration of pre-emption. Elements within the US administration who had been deeply engaged in the events of 1990–1991, such as Donald Rumsfeld, seemed now determined to 'finish' what had been started in 1991. Figures such as Paul Wolfowitz, who had served as Under-Secretary of

Defence for Policy during Desert Storm and shaped US policy, outlined their position on Iraq as self-confessed hawks who made clear their determination to achieve regime change in Baghdad. To what extent this aligned with the broader goals of the GWOT, the notion of threat to American security or elements such as economic and strategic considerations and ambitions as they related to the Middle East, would begin to come clear as the case for military action against Iraq was put by the US administration (along with British Prime Minister Tony Blair) to the court of world opinion. And much as the US wanted to carry a respectable body of international support with them, especially in the Islamic world, the bottom line appeared to be that if their traditional friends could not or would not help them (including a largely unconvinced UN Security Council) they would do the job themselves.[5]

At first it appeared that old alliances would endorse the US spearhead against Iraq. Through astute diplomatic endeavour the US and UK were able to secure a unanimous UN Security Council Resolution 1441 on 8 November 2002, in which the UN stipulated that Iraq must disarm, with provision for further UN action in case of incompliant Iraqi behaviour. The resolution was designed to kick-start the UN weapons inspections and disarmament process that had halted in 1998. The other dimension to this was to increase pressure for the maintenance of the UN sanctions regime against Iraq. UN data itself demonstrated that the sanctions, or rather (as some would argue) how they had been implemented by the Iraqi regime, had made conditions for ordinary Iraqis similar to those in a poorly resourced refugee camp. But, in the event, SCR 1441 would not be the 'green light' for military action that many in the Anglo-American camp believed it to be. Encouraged by the adoption of SCR 1441 the case for war was being furiously constructed in Washington and London, with regime change, weapons of mass destruction, human rights abuses, and other issues cited as reasons for seeking a pre-emptive conflict on Iraq and on the regime of Saddam Hussein. As diplomatic pressure grew and UN Security Council members such as France and Russia remained unconvinced by the case for war against Iraq, Dr Hans Blix, heading the UN weapons inspection team, also asked for more time. Yet by early March 2003 Britain and the US (along with other much smaller contingent Allied forces) were strategically located in the Middle East, with only the reluctance of Turkey to allow a US military presence hampering the war plans. At the UN the failure to obtain the necessary votes dissuaded Britain and the US from pursuing a Security Council resolution sanctioning military action in the name of the United Nations.

By 17 March 2003 preparations for war were well advanced and the prospect of sustaining peace in the Arab Gulf waned as UN personnel were ordered out of Iraq. Thousands of British and American troops took up positions in northern Kuwait, diplomats packed their bags and the massed ranks of the international press corps arrived in Doha and Kuwait City. Whether war would be short or long, bring the region to the brink of international crisis, lead to the toppling of regimes and the apogee of American power in the Middle East were all questions that were then unanswerable. There were fears that if Saddam Hussein possessed capability to engage weapons of mass destruction of a biological or chemical variety, then he would – the same fears precisely which were expressed over a decade earlier as the land war of February 1991 got underway. There were worries that America would end up engaged in a long-term conflict that would become increasingly unpopular at home, in which their military superiority would be undermined by local guerrilla tactics as had happened in Vietnam. There was a conviction in some quarters that a war on Iraq would do more to engender conflict in the Middle East – and from the Middle East, as perpetrated by terrorist elements – than ever before. This vision was outlined by the Vatican, which had declared:

> One can foresee the destabilisation of the entire Middle East because the more politicised Islamic masses, which already harbour a deep hate for the West, will see it as an act of war against Islam and against Arab and Muslim countries . . . The gravest consequence of a war against Iraq, however, would be a flare-up of terrorism against the United States and against allied Western countries.[6]

On 19 March 2003 the US took the initiative, launching missile strikes against targets in Baghdad, and in the first weeks of the war Allied military gains were made at some cost to the civilian population and to Iraqi military conscripts. There was a moment of disquiet in the second week of the war when it appeared that after taking Umm Qasr and Basra to the south of the country that military victory would not be swift. In reality there was a military pause before the assault on Baghdad. Qualms of a Stalingrad meets Baghdad, however, failed to materialize as the Iraqi defence disintegrated, with even allegedly elite units refusing to fight – the only determined opposition coming from Ba'ath party irregular units and some foreign Arab fighters. The regime elite seemed to evaporate literally overnight between 9 and 10 April, most tellingly symbolized by the overnight disappearance of the Iraqi Information Minister Mohammed Sahaf, the infamous voice of the regime. Even as Baghdad burned before his eyes and with US tanks less than a kilometre away, he announced to the global media that the city was safe from American hands. He had labelled the British and US leadership 'an international gang of criminal bastards, blood-sucking bastards, ignorant imperialists, losers and fools'. With the fall of Baghdad a few hours later, and the capitulation of the northern cities of Mosul, Takrit (the hometown of Saddam Hussein and many others in the regime) and Irbil within the week, military war was all but over.

Yet the fall of Baghdad, the capture of Kirkuk and the end of the regime of Saddam Hussein did not mean that the campaign had successfully run its course. Its repercussions in the Middle East were keenly felt. First, the implications of regime change pursued and achieved by America began to sink in. As David Frum, a former presidential speechwriter, noted: 'an American-led overthrow of Saddam Hussein . . . would put America more wholly in charge of the region than any power since the Ottomans, or maybe the Romans'.[7] Indeed, the sense that America was enjoying unprecedented authority over a number of regimes in the Middle East was overwhelming, with important implications for future conflicts and peacemaking. Within weeks of the fall of Baghdad the American spotlight was falling on Damascus with demands on Bashar al-Assad to crack down on certain elements. Then there was news that American troops would now be deployed out of Saudi Arabia, with many cynics pointing to Iraq as the new location for a US military presence in the Gulf. One conflict in particular, the Palestinian–Israeli dimension of the Arab–Israeli conflict, would once again come to the forefront of many minds in the region. The extent of power, as expressed in American hands, would now assume new dimensions.

A significant casualty of the 11 September attacks has been what then remained of the Middle East peace process (MEPP). Before September 2001 the second Palestinian uprising or Intifada, as we discussed in Chapter 2, had erupted. Palestinian violent resistance to the continued occupation of the West Bank and the hopeless stalemate in the MEPP was met by increasingly aggressive Israeli government military actions leading to unprecedented, mostly civilian casualties. Palestinian suicide bombers were becoming a familiar phenomenon, inflicting horrific carnage mostly against Israeli civilians – these acts inevitably leading to instant military retaliation.

Then came 11 September. The Israeli government, sensing a major tactical advantage, was quick to align Israel with the US in the war against terrorism. Palestinian political violence was increasingly conflated with the threat posed by al-Qaeda.[8] Israel, and the powerful Israeli lobby in the US, enthusiastically embraced and endorsed a simplistic view prevalent mostly on the American (and Israeli) Right that indiscriminately lumped together all kinds of dissident elements, mostly with Islamic connections and, for the main part, Arabs. As Camille Mansour has put it: 'Sharon immediately concluded that the new situation allowed him to claim that he was in the front line against terrorism. He now had *carte blanche* to set the rules of the game in the Palestinian–Israeli sphere . . . while loudly proclaiming that Arafat was Israel's Bin Laden.'[9] The most striking manifestation of Israeli policy post-11 September was the effort to marginalize Yasser Arafat and to degrade his security apparatus. Later Sharon tried to drive him into exile. From December until early May 2002 Israeli tanks besieged Arafat, confining him to his office complex in Ramallah. Islamist suicide bombings only increased in attacks against Israelis. Punitive Israeli airstrikes targeted his security forces and destroyed much of the PA's infrastructure. At the same time the Israelis demanded that the neutered Palestinian authorities rein in radical elements like Hamas and Islamic Jihad. In pursuing these tough tactics Ariel Sharon appeared to be acting with US acquiescence if not active support. On the Palestinian side suicide attacks deep into Israel and guerrilla raids on Jewish settlements and military outposts increased as part of the spiral of violence and counter-violence.

These conflagrations, covered on prime-time television, forced a reluctant US intervention in the form of Colin Powell, the US Secretary of State. This high profile regional swing was a watershed for the Bush administration with regard to the Palestinian–Israeli conflict. The US had adopted a hands-off approach to conflict management rather than resolution.[10] The Israeli reoccupation of the West Bank in April 2002 changed that. Many Arab capitals erupted in anti-Israeli and anti-US demonstrations in support of the Palestinians. The potential for destabilization forced the US to act. As far as many in the administration were concerned, the MEPP, despite its complete collapse, was less a priority than dealing with Iraq. But even the hard liners realized there was no hope of any Arab support for a new confrontation with Baghdad – even from traditional friends in the region – unless it could be seen to be actively involved in reviving the peace process. How even-handed the US was really mattered little. The onus was inevitably placed on the Palestinians to undertake a series of changes and reforms (some much needed) in a climate of daily Israeli measures against their civilian population. In the spring of 2003 the promise of a road map for peace was announced by the US. This built on the American-supported UN Security Council Resolution 1397,[11] which for the first time specifically endorsed a 'vision' of a Palestinian state alongside an Israeli one. In Bush's words, the vision he had outlined is one

> of a day when two states, Israel and Palestine, will live side by side in peace and security. I called upon all parties in the Middle East to abandon old hatreds and to meet their responsibilities for peace. The Palestinian state must be a reformed and peaceful and democratic state that abandons forever the use of terror. The government of Israel, as the terror threat is removed and security improves, must take concrete steps to support the emergence of a viable and credible Palestinian state, and to work as quickly as possible toward a final status agreement. As

progress is made toward peace, settlement activity in the occupied territories must end.[12]

So to what extent, post-11 September, are there new 'lines in the sand' with regard to the prospects for conflict and peace in the Middle East? Will Middle Eastern and Western (as well as other) governments need to reorder their priorities dramatically in the light of the 'war against terrorism'? Lights still burn late in many capitals of Western Europe, the former Soviet bloc and the Middle East and beyond looking at this question, and have done since September 2001. Our judgement is that the attacks of 11 September 2001 have altered the balance of power in the Middle East, with the most immediate consequences being felt in Afghanistan, among radical Islamist elements, the Palestinian–Israeli matrix and Iraq. In the medium- to long-term, American re-engagement in the region, which has given preference to pre-emptive military rather than diplomatic power, has major implications for relations within the region as well as for other international actors. There is now much more emphasis on security issues such as military training, sale of sophisticated defence equipment and the exchange of counter-terrorist intelligence with friendly countries. Arms sales, trading and militarization of the region is unlikely to decline. There may well be a realignment of the American military presence; Iraq may well be the route out of Saudi Arabia for US forces, but it is highly unlikely to be scaled down. Whether this results in conflict prevention of a major order, but the promotion of localized conflicts within states, it is difficult to predict. One outcome, however, is that bilateral and multilateral involvement by Western governments in aid programmes aimed at alleviating poverty in the poorer Arab countries will not be substantially increased. Peace-building will be difficult to sustain under such conditions.

A major priority will be monitoring potential internal threat in those countries with close ties with the West where there is known to be sympathy for al-Qaeda and some of whose nationals have been involved in the terrorist network. Saudi Arabia is probably the most worrying case. Despite the tight control that the House of Saud maintains over its citizens there is a real threat from dissident elements with radical Islamist associations. Some of these will also reflect the schisms within Islam and the tensions that Saudi promotion of Wahabbi fundamentalist ideology has created within the Muslim domain. For it is not only young Saudi radicals who are turning to Islam out of disgust with their regime's close ties with the West – especially the US with its support for Israel – and out of despair at the inability of regimes like theirs effectively to help the Palestinians. Stories of corruption on a vast scale amongst the princely elite fuel similar emotions in a country where the economy is weak and unemployment is rising amongst a young workforce. There is some evidence that recent bomb outrages blamed on expatriates are the work of home-grown elements seeking to destabilize the country, and the bland assurances of senior Saudis that all is well are not convincing. Yet there is still a failure to grasp the fact that the absence of adequate political and social rights generally, especially in the context of close official ties with the West, encourages support for radical dissident elements in a number of 'moderate' Arab countries. Poverty, abuse of human rights, striving for security at the expense of liberty and an absence of democratic or pluralistic institutions promote the conditions for political violence and terrorism, and thus conflict.

The problem is that there is considerable ambivalence throughout the Arab world over the question of political liberalization. Many political elites recognize the need to allow more popular participation, if only as a political safety valve. But others who appear to be calling the shots, perhaps mindful of what happened to the Soviet Union after Gorbachev, are concerned that political liberalization or democracy will quickly undermine and even oust them from power. Indeed, evidence of opposition from Islamist groups influenced by philosophies that are also embraced by bin Laden may be used by some of these regimes as yet another pretext for resisting the democratic impulse expressed among their people. They may be genuinely anxious about the degree of fundamental opposition – from a variety of social forces and elements – to their rule and prefer repression to liberty. And it is not in the Gulf countries alone that ruling authorities have ordered security crackdowns on the grounds of tackling terrorism. But in less evidently autocratic regimes like Jordan, Morocco and Egypt threats, real or imaginary, have provided the pretext for new attacks on fundamental liberties.

Admittedly in the Gulf some cautious steps permitting participation in state legislatures were taken in the wake of the second Gulf war of 1990–1991. This can be considered as a form of internally driven conflict prevention by the ruling elite. There is also awareness, in such circles, of the importance of economic reform to meet the rising expectations of expanding populations. Yet support for economic liberalization and diversification away from total reliance on oil and gas and their derivatives have not proved either a resounding economic or political success.[13] In 2002 there was recognition in reports from organizations such as the UNDP and the World Economic Forum that the states of the Middle East risked further regional instability and conflict because of its failure to modernize. The natural resources of the region, including water, oil and gas have not effectively been harnessed. Corruption, stagnating economies, poor levels of basic education and high population growth rates (in some cases they are the highest in the world) generate conditions that undermine the prospects for peace and prosperity for the citizens of this region It was economic greed that motivated many past conflicts within the region, and they in turn were often linked to strategic considerations allied to external powers and actors. Additionally, there is a scepticism that economic reform policies, which were previously advocated and promoted throughout the late 1980s and 1990s, will work any better second time around. After Iraq there is a perception, rightly or wrongly, of the threat of Western military intervention to enforce regime change. Heavy hints about possible US-led action against such regimes as Syria and Iran inevitably could be a serious destabilizing factor should they become a consistent *leitmotif* of US rhetoric. And there will continue to be a dissonance between Western-led global capitalism and resistance to it within much of the region. The UNDP report was forthright in its conclusions, arguing that the refusal of political and other leaders in the region to grant women more rights, open up the political process, improve education and crack down on widespread corruption left it incapable of pulling itself out of a two-decade slump. Additionally, the geo-politics of the region, focused as they are on the negative recurrences of conflicts, have left little opportunity for policy-makers and bureaucrats to concentrate state resources and energies on growth, prosperity and peace. The example of Israel demonstrates this, for even with major economic assistance from the US in the form of direct aid and loans the Israeli economy has been driven into crisis as a result of conflict with its Palestinian neighbours, 11 September and the world-wide recession. A return to peace will promote economic recovery for Israel and help it regain global competitiveness. Regional peace will aid recovery even better. Indeed, it is worth remembering that the peace dividends for Israel, in terms of inward investment etc., from the Oslo Accords were higher than for any Arab party, and this imbalance needs to figure in the new equations for peace in the region. The asymmetry of power – political, economic or other – militates against a lasting peace.

In the current highly charged atmosphere it will need a major effort by the international community to revive any peace process. The grievances of the Palestinians and how they are redressed will remain the touchstone of how the Arabs view the policies of the West. A fair, just and comprehensive peace will do more than anything else to dissipate support for bin Laden and other extremist groups. Despite ambitions by British Prime Minister Tony Blair to lead the march for peace, or the agenda of other state actors such as France or Russia, it is only American leverage, pressure, military or diplomatic power than can transform the Palestinian–Israeli track. This is not, however, the same as applying such pressures in other zones or domains of conflict in the region. American leverage did not and is unlikely to work in Lebanon, nor in Algeria. Nor within its parameters as perceived at present can it hope to resolve the challenges arising from the wider manifestation of Islamist politics, including their extremist offshoots. The path to peace, rather than to that of military pacification, will have to be envisioned entirely differently.

Short glossary of terms and organizations

Aliyah Jewish immigration. The first Aliyah was between 1882 and 1884 and again between 1890 and 1891 when immigrants came to Palestine from Russia and Eastern Europe. Four further Aliyahs between 1905 and the 1930s were stimulated by events in Europe, the most significant being the rise of the Nazis in Germany.

Amal Groups of the Lebanese Resistance. An anti-Israeli Shi'a radical organization based in southern Lebanon founded by Imam Musa al Sadr in 1974. Post-1980 the Islamic section of Amal propagated Ayatollah Khomeini's views. It developed into Hizballah ('The party of God'). Amal enjoyed support from Syria and Iranian Hizballah, thus splitting the Shi'a radical movement in Lebanon into two rival groups.

Arab League The League of Arab States founded in 1947 by Egypt, Lebanon, Iraq, Syria, Transjordan, Yemen and Saudi Arabia. Since then Palestine and all independent Arab countries represented by the PLO have joined.

Ba'ath party From the Arabic for 'Renaissance'. A Pan Arab socialist party originating in Syria in 1947. It had considerable influence in Jordan, Lebanon and Iraq and came to power in both Syria and Iraq.

Black September Name given by Palestinians to events in Jordan in September 1970 which initiated a civil war leading to the defeat of the PLO leadership by King Hussein. Following the Palestinian defeat in Jordan Fatah created a terrorist organization of this name. It was responsible for the killing of the Jordanian Prime Minister in 1971 and of eleven Israeli athletes at the Munich Olympics in 1972.

Deir Yassin Palestinian village where, in April 1948, 245 Palestinian civilians, including women and children, were massacred by Zionist forces. Palestinians claim that this was an act of ethnic cleansing sanctioned by the new Israeli leadership to encourage Palestinians to flee. The majority of Israelis refute the Palestinian claim as propaganda.

Diaspora Originally referred to dispersion of Jews around the world following the destruction of Jerusalem by the Romans in AD 135. Now also applied to world-wide Palestinian communities exiled since the war of 1948.

Eisenhower Doctrine   Proclaimed by President Eisenhower in 1957 promising US assistance to Middle Eastern states threatened by 'International Communism'. Cited to justify US assistance to Jordan and military involvement in Lebanon in 1958. Ideological basis for US support for the Central Treaty Organisation (CENTO) involving Turkey, Iran and Pakistan.

Al Fatah   Reverse acronym from the Arabic **H**araka **T**ahriir **Fa**listiin, a movement to liberate Palestine. Established in 1957 and led by Yasser Arafat. Largest Palestinian movement.

Fatwa   Muslim edict issued by religious leaders.

Fedayeen   Arabic term for resistance forces, particularly those of the PLO.

Golan Heights   Strategically important highlands in Syria dominating the Sea of Galilee and the northern Jordan valley. Occupied by Israeli forces in 1967 and 'annexed' in 1981. The home of a number of Jewish settlements. Remains the main bone of contention between Syria and Israel.

Green Line   Line in Beirut dividing Christian and Muslim communities established during the civil war of 1975 to 1990. Also the armistice lines between Israel and neighbouring Arab countries drawn up in 1949 following the first Arab–Israeli war.

Gulf Co-operation Council (GCC)   Formed in May 1981 by the six Arab gulf monarchies of Saudi Arabia, Bahrain, Qatar, Oman, Kuwait and the United Arab Emirates. Framework for co-operation amongst the member states in a number of areas including defence and external relations.

Hamas   Name acronym from the Arabic *Harakat al-Muqawama al-Islamic*: 'Movement of the Islamic Resistance'. Radical Palestinian Islamic movement opposed to peace with Israel and to the Oslo Accords. Emerged during the **Intifada** and has conducted a number of terrorist attacks on Israelis including suicide bombings.

Halabja   Iraqi Kurdish area attacked by Iraq with chemical weapons in March 1988.

Hizballah (Party of God)   Lebanese Shi'ite radical organization. Rival of **Amal**. Enjoys financial backing from Iran. Mainly instrumental in enforcing the Israeli withdrawal from south Lebanon in 2000.

Intifada   Palestinian popular uprising that erupted in December 1987 against the Israeli occupation of Gaza and the West Bank.

Islamic Jihad   Name of Palestinian Islamist organization, which gave first impetus to the **Intifada** calling for a return to Islamic values as well as fighting Israel. Also name for members of Khomeini's Islamic Revolutionary Movement operating together with Amal and Hizballah from the Beqaa Valley in Lebanon under command of 'Council of Lebanon'.

Jihad   Means 'struggle'. Obligation of Muslims to engage in defensive battle in the face of foreign occupation or unjust rule.

Knesset   Israel's parliament.

Law of Return   Law passed by **Knesset** in 1950 giving Jews everywhere legal right of immigration to Israel.

Levant   Originally the Eastern Mediterranean landmass from Greece to Egypt. Levant meaning 'rising' (sun). Commonly refers to Syria and the Lebanon.

Likud party   Israeli right-wing parliamentary bloc formed in 1973.

Maghreb   'West' in Arabic. Used to describe the North African countries of Morocco, Algeria, Tunisia and Libya.

Majlis   Arabic (and Farsi) word meaning 'assembly'. Used for parliaments throughout the Arab World and in Iran.

Mandate   System of administration authorized by the League of Nations for former German colonies and Asian parts of the Ottoman Empire at the end of the First World War. Intended for the tutelage by the more advanced nations of peoples considered unready for independence. In the Middle East Britain was awarded the mandates for Palestine, Transjordan and Iraq; France for Syria and Lebanon.

Mossad   Israeli external intelligence service.

Nasserism   Arab nationalist sentiment focused on President Gamal Abdul Nasser of Egypt throughout the 1950s and 1960s as the main exponent of shaping a distinctive Arab identity and social progress.

Occupied Palestinian Territories   The areas occupied by Israel following the 1967 war: the **Golan Heights** taken from Syria (and annexed by Israel in1981); the West Bank conquered from Jordan; the Gaza Strip seized from Egyptian control, the Sinai Peninsular from Egypt and East Jerusalem from Jordan and illegally annexed in 1967.

Palestine Liberation Organization (PLO)   Founded in 1964, it is the umbrella organization for a number of Palestinian political and guerrilla organizations.

Palestinian National Authority (PNA)   Chaired by Yasser Arafat, it is the legislative and executive body responsible for exercising powers devolved to the autonomous Palestinian areas following the Oslo agreements with Israel.

Pan Arabism   Movement for Arab unity as one Arab nation.

Phalangist party (Kataib)   Main political party of the Maronite right with a history of fascist tendencies.

Republican Guard   Elite Iraqi troop unit which made possible the Ba'athist coup of Baghdad in 1968.

Sephardi   Commonly refers to Jews of Middle Eastern or North African origin.

South Lebanon Army   A Christian militia force which acted as an ally and proxy of Israel during its occupation of south Lebanon.

UNIFIL   United National Interim Force in Lebanon established in 1978 as a result of UN Resolution 425 as a peacekeeping force.

Zionism   Political ideology for the establishment of a Jewish state.

Notes

Introduction

1 Orientalism refers to the tradition of antipathy and hostility to the Middle East and Muslim world that grew out of the political motivations of colonial intervention in the Middle East. The debate about orientalism is discussed further in Chapter 4. See E. Said, *Orientalism*, Harmondsworth: Penguin, 1995 (second edition).

2 S. Bromley, *Rethinking the Middle East*, Cambridge: Polity, 1994, p. 116.

3 Arthur Balfour was the British Foreign Secretary who in 1917 issued a declaration announcing support for the Zionist cause in Palestine. See Chapters 1 and 2 for further explanation (also Notes Chapter 1).

4 S. Fischer, D. Rodrik, E. Tuma (eds), *The Economics of Middle East Peace: Views from the Region*, Cambridge, Mass.: MIT Press, 1993, p. 2.

5 E. Picard, 'Arab military in politics', in G. Luciani (ed.), *The Arab State*, London: Routledge, 1990, p. 192. According to A. H. Cordesman the 'Middle East remains the most militarised region in the world by virtually every measure of effort'. A. H. Cordesman, *The Military Balance in the Middle East – An Overview*, Washington: Centre for Security and International Studies, 1998, p. 3.

6 A. Richards and J. Waterbury, *A Political Economy of the Middle East*, Boulder, Colo.: Westview Press, 1990, p. 359.

7 F. Halliday, 'The Middle East at the millennial turn', in *Middle East Report*, Winter 1999, p. 5.

Chapter 1

1 A. Gresch and D. Vidal, *An A to Z of the Middle East*, London: Zed Books, 1990, p. 210.

2 E. Sahliyeh, 'Beyond the cold war: the superpowers and the Arab–Israeli conflict', in S. L. Speigel (ed.), *Conflict Management in the Middle East*, Boulder, Colo.: Westview Press, 1992, p. 381.

3 Many members of south Lebanon's Shi'a population had originally welcomed the Israelis, believing they would rid Lebanon of the PLO which by that point had not only become embroiled in Lebanon's civil war but was universally accused of exacerbating and creating new dimensions to it.

4 E. Monroe, *Britain's Moment in the Middle East*, London: Chatto & Windus, 1963, p. 66.

5 The Balfour Declaration issued on 2 November 1917 outlined a British government pledge to support the Zionists in which it announced 'his Majesty's Government views with favour the establishment in Palestine of a national home for the Jewish people'. The League of Nations mandate for Palestine awarded to the British government in 1923 urged Britain in Palestine to 'be responsible for placing the country under such political, administrative and economic conditions as will secure the establishment of a Jewish national home'.

6 M. Rodinson, *Israel and the Arabs*, Harmondsworth: Penguin, 1982, p. 45.

7 M. Gilbert, *The Arab–Israeli Conflict, Its History in Maps*, London: Weidenfeld & Nicolson, 1984 (fourth edition), p. 46.

8 King Hussein of Jordan, for example, was pressurized into a war that he knew he couldn't win. See B. Milton-Edwards and P. Hinchcliffe, *Jordan, a Hashemite Legacy*, Reading: Harwoods, 2000.

9 The main principle behind SCR 242 was 'Land for Peace' in which it was hoped that Israel could be persuaded to trade the Arab land it occupied for the promise of recognition and peace from its Arab neighbours.

10 T. Fraser, *The Arab–Israeli Conflict*, Basingstoke: Macmillan, 1995, p. 86.

11 D. Gerner, *One Land, Two People, The Conflict over Palestine*, Boulder, Colo.: Westview Press, 1994, p. 120.

12 D. Gilmour, *Dispossessed: The Ordeal of the Palestinians*, London: Sphere Books, 1980, p. 224.

13 The extent of Israeli losses in Lebanon became a major factor in motivating public opinion in favour of a withdrawal. Since 1982 more than 1,000 Israeli soldiers lost their lives as a result of the occupation of south Lebanon. Their local proxy, the South Lebanon Army, also incurred losses at the hands of Hizballah resistance fighters and others which ran into several hundreds.

Chapter 2

1 M. Tessler, *A History of the Arab–Israeli Conflict*, Bloomington and Indianapolis: Indiana University Press, 1994, p. xi.

2 A. Gresch and D. Vidal, *An A to Z of the Middle East*, London: Zed, 1990, p. 221.

3 D. Gerner, *One Land, Two Peoples, The Conflict over Palestine*, Boulder, Colo.: Westview Press, 1994, p. 15.

4 E. Karsh (ed.), *Between War and Peace, Dilemmas of Israeli Security*, London: Frank Cass, 1996, p. 1.

5 See: I. Pappe, *The Making of the Arab–Israeli Conflict 1947–1951*, London: I.B. Tauris, 1994. Also B. Morris, *1948 and After, Israel and the Palestinians*, Oxford: Clarendon Press, 1994.

6 By 1999 there were 195 Israeli settlements in the West Bank (including Jerusalem) and the Gaza Strip. Since 1967 the Israeli authorities have confiscated 750,000 acres of land from the 1.5 million acres in the West Bank and Gaza Strip. According to Miftah, the 'very existence of Israeli settlements is a direct violation of internationally binding agreements and regulations; international humanitarian law explicitly prohibits the occupying state to make permanent changes that are not, in the first place, intended to benefit the population of the occupied'. www.miftah.org/factsheets/sheets/settlements.html

7 See: Y. Sayigh, *Armed Struggle and the Search for a State*, Oxford: Oxford University Press, 1980.
8 Ibid., p. 624.
9 See E. Ya'ari and Ze'ev Schiff, *Intifada, the Palestinian Uprising – Israel's Third Front*, New York: Simon and Schuster, 1989, pp. 263–64. Also D. Peretz, *Intifada, The Palestinian Uprising*, Boulder, Colo.: Westview Press, 1990.
10 R. Khalidi, *Palestinian Identity, the Construction of Modern Consciousness*, New York: Columbia University Press, 1997, p. 201.

Chapter 3

1 Chomsky goes on to remark that, 'While it is true that the US would not tolerate Soviet moves that threatened to provide the USSR with a significant role in Middle East oil production or distribution, this has rarely been a realistic concern – which is not to say that ideologists have not come to believe the fantasies they conjure up to serve other needs'. N. Chomsky, *Fateful Triangle: The United States, Israel and the Palestinians*, London: Pluto Press, 1999 (updated edition), p. 17.
2 M. Rodinson, *Israel and the Arabs*, Harmondsworth: Penguin, 1968, p. 115.
3 D. Lesch (ed.), *The Middle East and the United States, a Historical and Political Reassessment*, Boulder, Colo.: Westview Press, 1996, p. 2.
4 Quoted by B. Reich, 'The United States and Israel: the nature of the special relationship', in D. Lesch (ed.), *The Middle East and the United States, a Historical and Political Reassessment*, Boulder, Colo.: Westview Press, 1996, p. 233.
5 These figures along with others are quoted in A. Richards and J. Waterbury, *A Political Economy of the Middle East*, Boulder, Colo.: Westview Press, 1990, p. 362.
6 N. Chomsky, op. cit., p. 19.
7 E. Alin, 'US Policy and military intervention in the 1958 Lebanon crisis', in D. Lesch (ed.), *The Middle East and the United States, a Historical and Political Reassessment*, Boulder, Colo.: Westview Press, 1996, p. 160.
8 Ibid., pp. 148–62.
9 J. Stork, N. Aruri, and F. Moughrabi, *Reagan and the Middle East*, Belmont, Mass.: AAUG, 1983, p. 31.
10 As Reich notes, Reagan actively courted Israel, 'he saw Israel as an important ally and an asset in the struggle against the Soviet Union . . . [and] the US-Israeli relationship during the eight years Reagan held office was generally characterized by close positive ties'. B. Reich, 'The United States and Israel: the nature of the special relationship', in D. Lesch (ed.), *The Middle East and the United States, a Historical and Political Reassessment*, Boulder, Colo.: Westview Press, 1996, p. 238.
11 D. McLaurin, *The Middle East in Soviet Policy*, London: D.C. Heath, 1975, p. 126.
12 A. Dawisha and K. Dawisha (eds), *The Soviet Union in the Middle East: Policies and Perspectives*, London: Heinemann, 1982, p. 77.
13 G. Mirsky, 'The Soviet perception of the US threat', in D. Lesch (ed.), *The Middle East and the United States, a Historical and Political Reassessment*, Boulder, Colo.: Westview Press, 1996, p. 409. See also A. Dawisha and K. Dawisha (eds), *The Soviet Union in the Middle East: Policies and Perspectives*, London: Heinemann, 1982.

14   R. Fisk, 'Myth of "Pax-Americana"'
     http://www.thenation.com/issue/961014/1014fisk.htm 1996, p. 1.

Chapter 4

 1   S. Huntington, 'The clash of civilisations?', in *Foreign Affairs*, Summer 1993, p. 25.
 2   See E. Said, *Orientalism*, Harmondsworth: Penguin, 1995 (second edition).
 3   E. Said, *Covering Islam: How the Media and Experts Determine How we See the Rest of the World*, London: Vintage, 1997, p. 163.
 4   J. Miller, 'The challenge of radical Islam', in *Foreign Affairs*, Vol. 72:2, Spring 1993, p. 33.
 5   B. Lewis, 'The roots of Muslim rage', in *Atlantic Monthly*, No. 266:3, February 1990, p. 53.
 6   J. Esposito, *The Islamic Threat: Myth or Reality?*, Oxford: Oxford University Press, 1992, p. 139.
 7   For more on the cause of the Algerian crisis see M. Willis, *The Islamist Challenge in Algeria: A Political History*, Reading, Mass.: Ithaca Press, 1996. Also G. Joffe (ed.), *North Africa: Nation, State, and Religion*, London: Routledge, 1993.
 8   A. Tahi, 'Algeria's democratisation process: a frustrated hope', in *Third World Quarterly*, Vol. 16:2, 1995, p. 219.
 9   H. Amirouche, 'Algeria's Islamist Revolution: the people versus democracy?', in *Middle East Policy*, 1 January 1998, p. 2.
10   D. Rapoport, 'Fear and trembling: terrorism in three religious traditions', in *American Political Science Review*, Vol. 78, 1984, pp. 662–84.
11   A. Taheri, *Holy Terror, The Inside Story of Islamic Terrorism*, London: Sphere Books, 1987, p. 1.

Chapter 5

 1   From Albert Hourani, *Political Society in Lebanon: A Historical Introduction*, Centre for International Studies, Cambridge, Mass.: MIT, 1986.
 2   For greater historical detail on pre-1920 Lebanon see M. Yapp, *The Making of the Modern Near East*, London and New York: Longman, 1987, pp. 128–37. See also the clear and concise essay by Y. Choueiri on the history of the Lebanon in *Middle East and North Africa 2000*, London: Europa, 1999, pp. 776–77.
 3   F. Massoulié describes this episode in *Middle East Conflicts*, New York: Interlink Publishing, 1999, p. 137.
 4   'Little Lebanon' in 1913 had a population of 415,000 of which 330,000 (79 per cent) were Christians. By 1923 'Greater Lebanon' – the area of the present state – had over 600,000 of whom 47 per cent were Muslims. The smaller entity was largely Christian-Druze whilst the post-1920 mandated territory was a patchwork of religious communities and included the largely Sunni coastal towns and the Shi'ite Beqaa valley.
 5   A recent estimated breakdown (1998) puts Shi'a Muslims at 33 per cent, Sunni Muslims 20 per cent, Maronite Christian 20 per cent, Greek Orthodox 8.3 per cent, Druze 8 per cent, Greek Catholic 6.0 per cent, Armenian Christian 4 per cent, other 0.7 per cent. Source: C. C. Held, *Middle East Patterns, Places, Peoples and Politics*, Boulder, Colo.: Westview Press, p. 221.

6   Farid el-Khazen describes how Lebanon's 'plural society' differs from other communally divided countries such as Belgium, Switzerland, Canada, the former Czechoslovakia, Malaysia, Sri Lanka, India and the Sudan. An excellent book for someone wishing to study Lebanon in more depth. F. el-Khazen, *The Breakdown of the State in Lebanon*, London and New York: I.B.Tauris, 2000, (especially pp. 32–33).

7   So sensitive did the question of population become – especially to Christians who realized that they were being steadily overtaken by Muslims – that 1932 was the last official census undertaken by the Lebanese government. Any new census would certainly demonstrate a marked decline in the Christian communities.

8   D. Stoten, *A State without a Nation*, Durham: University of Durham Centre for Middle Eastern and Islamic Studies, 1992. See especially the concluding chapter (pp. 78–82).

9   For further reading on pre-1957 Lebanese politics see M. E. Yapp, *The Near East Since the First World War*, Harlow: Longman, 1996, pp. 110–15.

10 Farid el-Khazen, *The Communal Pact of National Identities*, Oxford: Centre for Lebanese Studies, 1991. See pp. 5–7 for more detail on the negotiations also involving the French, British and Egyptians which led to the adoption of the pact.

11 F. Massoulié, op. cit., p. 139.

12 M. E. Yapp, op. cit., p. 265.

13 The civil war has spawned many books, some of the more graphic by Western victims of the spate of kidnapping (see Bibliography for further reading). For a well written and atmospheric (if journalistic) account see Robert Fisk, *Pity the Nation*, London: Athenaeum, 1990.

14 G. Luciani and G. Salamé. *The Arab State*, London: Routledge, 1990, p. 402.

15 UNRWA statistics in 1998 show a figure of 364,551 registered Palestinian refugees. Their situation is in marked contrast to the 1.3 million in Jordan, many of whom are fully integrated into Jordanian society.

Chapter 6

1   There is a wide variation of estimates of the Kurdish population world-wide. P. G. Kreyenbroek and S. Sperl (eds), *The Kurds. A Contemporary Overview*, London and New York: Routledge, 1992 puts the figure at 19 million. The estimate of 26 million comes from David McDowell's *The Kurds*, London: Minority Rights Group International, 1996. Accuracy is difficult given the tendency of Kurdish nationalists to inflate the figure and for host governments to minimize the statistics (or up to recently in the case of Turkey to disallow the use of the label 'Kurd' at all). McDowell's breakdown on page 7 of the MRGI publication is likely to be as accurate as any.

2   Some scholars have argued that the Kurds are a nation and rather more than an ethnic group, although one without a state. G. M. Kirisci and K. Winrow (eds) discuss this in *The Kurdish Question and Turkey. An Example of a Trans-state Ethnic Conflict*, London and Portland: Frank Cass, 1998. This is a very useful and balanced account of the Kurds within Turkey.

3   Page 6 of the MRGI report refers to the fact that modern Kurdish nationalists tend to exaggerate the exact extent of historical Kurdistan. In some areas 'claimed' by the Kurds, such as the environs of Irbil (which has an almost exclusively Kurdish population), Arabs have always been in a large majority.

4 Kirisci and Winrow, op. cit., p. 26. They point to the possible sense of multiple identity felt by some Kurdish Turks (or Turkish Kurds!) depending on their tribal identity, primary dialect group, religion or social class. The context would often determine which identity such persons might wish to stress at any one time.

5 The issue of Sèvres and the aspirations of the Kurds is discussed in great detail in McDowell's seminal work *A Modern History of the Kurds*, London and New York: I.B. Tauris, 1997. This is probably the best comprehensive historical study of the Kurds in English and is easily accessible to the general reader. McDowell has considerable sympathy for the Kurds and his objectivity is occasionally open to challenge.

6 According to McDowell, recent research has uncovered such an idea emanating from Ataturk (see Kreyenbroek and Sperl, op. cit., p. 18).

7 In safeguarding the interests of a 'recognized minority' the British had undertaken to replace their own officials with Kurds and to maintain Kurdish as the language of administration and of education. Pages 23 and 24 of the MRGI report are an excellent and concise summary of this period.

8 Translated as 'those who face death'. A romantic title for the Kurdish nationalist fighters!

9 Accurate figures for Kurdish losses at this time are impossible to obtain. According to R. Lawless in his 'Essay on Iraqi History' in *The Middle East and North Africa 2000*, London: Europa, 1999, pp. 522–23, over 3,000 out of 4,000 Kurdish villages were razed during the Iraq–Iran war alone and one-third of the Kurdish area depopulated. The figure of 200,000 dead comes from MRGI report – from Kurdish sources – and may be exaggerated. Other authorities quote 100,000 plus.

10 Quoted in the MRGI report, p. 18.

11 The then Minister of Justice is quoted in the MRGI report as saying 'I believe that the Turk must be the only lord, the only master of this country. Those who are not of pure Turkish stock can only have one right in this country, the right to be servants and slaves' (Mahmut Esat Bozhurt, 22 September 1930).

Chapter 7

1 These estimates are from M. E. Yapp, *The Near East Since the First World War*, Harlow: Longman, 1996.

2 Ibid., pp. 427–32 are a readable and succinct account of the war. Professor Yapp's conclusions are particularly convincing. Indeed his history makes an excellent supplementary companion to this work.

3 Pirouz Mojtahed-Zahed, *Security and Territoriality in the Persian Gulf*, Richmond, Surrey: Curzon, 1999. Despite some pro-Iranian partiality, pp. 44–52 provide good background to the Iraq–Iran confrontation of 1969 to 1975.

4 Richard Lawless, 'Essay on Iraqi History', in *The Middle East and North Africa 2000*, London: Europa, 1999. See pp. 549–56 for a detailed but concise account of the build up to and main events of the war.

5 Lawless (ibid.) claims that 'most commentators' agree that Saddam Hussein was seeking the toppling of the Iranian regime as the primary war aim. By contrast Bassam Tibi in his *Conflict and War in the Middle East*, Basingstoke: Macmillan, 1998 (p. 156) convincingly outlines a range of Iraqi objectives on the lines we have described in this chapter. See also Yapp, op. cit., p. 428. For

an admittedly prejudiced Iranian perspective see Farhang Rajaee (ed.), *The Iran– Iraq War. The Politics of Aggression*, Gainesville: University Press of Florida, 1993. For a differing view see L. Freedman and E. Karsh, *The Gulf Conflict 1990–1991*, London and Boston: Faber & Faber, 1993. They argue that Saddam was reacting to Iranian provocation and had very limited war aims confined to deterring Khomeini and occupying small areas of Iran of strategic importance for Iraq's access to the Gulf.

6 B. Tibi, op. cit., pp. 156–57. He coins the phrase 'potent socio-psychological synthesis between Shia Islam and Persian nationalism' to describe the unifying force in Iran in the early stages of the Gulf War.

7 In addition to Lawless' coherent account of the ebb and flow of war (Note 4) there is a detailed annotated chronology in *The Longman Companion to the Middle East Since 1914*, London and New York: Longman, 1998, pp. 145–48. A. Ehteshami and G. Nonneman's (eds) comprehensive study *War and Peace in the Gulf*, Reading, Mass.: Ithaca Press, 1991 also annexes an excellent chronology. This is one of the best studies for the specialist reader.

8 Lawless quotes a *Washington Post* report to the effect that the Chinese sold Iraq arms worth $3,100 million between 1981 and 1985. Sales to Iran were $575 million in the same period. Soviet supplies to Iraq included SS-12 missiles. These were more sophisticated than the Chinese 'silk worm' missiles used by the Iranians, which basically used the same technology as in the German V2 rockets in 1944–45. For comprehensive statistics on arms transfers see especially Chapter 4 of *War and Peace in the Gulf* (op. cit.).

9 It emerged in November 1986 that despite a formal position of neutrality the US had supplied arms to Iran – three shipments since 1985. Washington had been strongly discouraging any arms transfers to Iran. The primary purpose was to enlist Iranian help for freeing American hostages held by Shi'a militant groups in Lebanon. One further scandalous aspect was that it transpired that profits from these consignments were secretly siphoned off by officials to fund the Nicaraguan rebels – the Contras – thus evading congressional prohibitions on such operations. This, together with allegations that the CIA had provided intelligence (much of it said to be falsified) to both combatants (blamed by the Iraqis for the loss of Fao), raised doubts as to the aims of US policy towards the war. One theory was that Washington was trying to ensure that neither side could gain a decisive advantage.

10 For more detail about the Kurdish involvement in the Gulf War see Chapter 6. A detailed if partisan account of the chemical attacks on Halabja and subsequently in the campaign are given in D. McDowell's *A Modern History of the Kurds*, London and New York: I. B. Tauris, 1997.

11 Said Aburish, *Saddam Hussein. The Politics of Revenge*, London: Bloomsbury, 2000 gives an interesting analysis of Saddam's motives and conduct of the war (pp. 190–222). Very anti the Iraqi leader but a good read nonetheless.

Chapter 8

1 M. E. Yapp's *The Near East Since the First World War*, Harlow: Longman, 1996 gives a good overview. Pages 499–501 cover the run up to the Kuwait crisis.

2 For a detailed account of the 'new thinking' in the Soviet Union up to, during and immediately after the Kuwait crisis see Chapter 3 of R. O. Freedman's *The*

Middle East after Iraq's invasion of Kuwait, Gainesville: University Press of Florida, 1993. This book also has excellent essays on the policies pursued by the other main players and the opening chapter, 'The Gulf War. A political and military assessment', is a valuable analysis of the conflict.

3 For examinations of this argument see A. Ehteshami and G. Nonneman (eds) *War and Peace in the Gulf*, Reading, Mass.: Ithaca Press, 1991. Pages 71–75 are an especially concise and clear account of the developing crisis in 1990. The whole book is a very worthwhile and accessible (to the general reader) analysis of the war including documents such as Iraqi statements and UN Resolutions. For more detail of the war itself and the immediate aftermath see L. Freedman and E. Karsh, *The Gulf Conflict 1990–1991*, London and Boston: Faber & Faber, 1993.

4 According to Ehteshami and Nonneman (op. cit.) Iraq's indebtedness to Saudi Arabia by August 1990 amounted to $34 billion and to Kuwait to about $15 billion. This included the proceeds of oil sold by both countries on behalf of Iraq as well as the huge debts run up during the war with Iran.

5 In June 1981 Israeli war planes attacked a building complex outside Baghdad suspected to be an Iraqi nuclear installation.

6 This was Farzad Bazoft, on assignment for the *Observer* newspaper, who had been arrested near a defence industry complex in March 1990. His subsequent trial and execution for spying led to a marked deterioration of relations with the UK.

7 An excellent analysis of Iraqi conduct and motivation is in Bassam Tibi's *Conflict and War in the Middle East*, Basingstoke: Macmillan, 1998 (2nd edn), especially Chapter 9.

8 See for example Said K. Aburish, *Saddam Hussein. The Politics of Revenge*, London: Bloomsbury, 2000. His account of the Arab League summit of 30 and 31 May 1990 illuminates vividly the attitudes of the main players as the crisis deepened.

9 There are persistent reports that although the Kuwaitis showed some inclination towards considering Iraqi demands, Sheikh Sa'ad bin Abdullah, the Kuwaiti Crown Prince, had been very insulting about Saddam personally, thus triggering the invasion.

10 See for example Sami Yousef, 'The Iraqi–US War: a conspiracy theory' in Haim Bresheeth and Nira Yuval-Davis (eds), *The Gulf War and The New World Order*, London and New Jersey: Zed Books, 1991. Like some other writers (mostly Arab) Yousef believes that Washington lured Saddam into attacking Kuwait so that the US could set him up as the regional 'bogeyman'.

11 April Glaspie told one of the authors that she felt that she had left Saddam Hussein in no doubt that the US government would not accept Iraqi aggression against Kuwait. Conversation with Hinchcliffe in Amman in July 1996.

12 Four members of the Arab League had sent troops to Kuwait in 1961 to take over from the British forces that had responded to a request for assistance from newly-independent Kuwait following a claim by Iraq of sovereignty over the Emirate. The Arab League's principal motivation was to end the embarrassment of having troops from the former colonial power intervening in the region rather than facing a real prospect of fighting Iraq. A subsidiary factor was the contest for leadership in the Arab world between Baghdad and Cairo; the United Arab Republic strongly supported British claims that the Iraqis had designs on Kuwait. An excellent account is given in M. M. Alani, *Operation*

Vantage. British Military Intervention in Kuwait 1961, Surbiton: Laam Press, 1990.

13 The claim to Kuwait had been maintained by successive Iraqi regimes. Kuwait was an artificial neo-colonialist creation of the British carved out of the Ottoman province of Basra, which became Iraq and rightfully formed part of its territory. This argument was broadened to include all colonial imposed frontiers as serving imperialist interests and being obstacles to the Holy Grail of Pan Arab unity.

14 See Ehteshami and Nonneman (op. cit.), especially pp. 81–83.

15 George Bush, the US President, appeared to encourage these uprisings when addressing the Iraqi people following the post-war ceasefire. But the uprisings were genuinely spontaneous, taking advantage of the spectacular defeat of the Iraqi armed forces.

16 Iraqi military casualties were about 35,000; 370 coalition soldiers died, a high proportion from 'friendly fire'.

Chapter 9

1 A. Arian, *Politics in Israel, The Second Generation*, London: Chatham House Press, 1989 (revised edn), pp. 218–19.

2 For further discussion see J. Goodhand and D. Hulme, 'From wars to complex political emergencies: understanding conflict and peace-building in the new world order', in *Third World Quarterly*, Vol. 20:1, 1999, pp. 13–26.

3 See: K. Rupesinghe (ed.), *Conflict Transformation*, Basingstoke: Macmillan, 1995. Also L. Kriesberg, T. A. Northrup, and S. J. Thorson (eds), *Intractable Conflicts and their Transformation*, Syracuse: Syracuse University Press, 1989.

4 K. Rupesinghe, *Civil Wars, Civil Peace – An Introduction to Conflict Resolution*, London: Pluto Press, 1998, p. 115. For further debate of conflict resolution theory see C. Mitchell and M. Banks, *Handbook of Conflict Resolution, the Analytical Problem-solving Approach*, London: Pinter, 1996, and L. Kriesberg, *Constructive Conflicts, from Escalation to Resolution*, Lanham, Md.: Rowman & Littlefield, 1998.

5 F. Halliday, 'The Middle East at the millennial turn', in *Middle East Report*, Winter 1999, No. 213, p. 6.

6 See: J. Maila, 'The Ta'if Accord: an evaluation', in D. Collings (ed.), *Peace for Lebanon: From War to Reconstruction*, Boulder, Colo.: Lynne Rienner, 1994.

7 Z. Flamhaft, *Israel on the Road to Peace – Accepting the Unacceptable*, Boulder, Colo.: Westview Press, 1996, p. 183.

8 A. Abu Odeh, *Jordanians, Palestinians and the Hashemite Kingdom in the Middle East Peace Process*, Washington: USIP, 1999, p. 274.

9 D. Makovsky, *Making Peace with the PLO, the Rabin Government's Road to the Oslo Accord*, Boulder, Colo.: Westview Press, 1996, p. 22.

10 F. Halliday, op. cit., p. 5.

11 B. Milton-Edwards, 'Iraq, past, present and future: a thoroughly modern mandate', in *History and Policy*, May 2003, pp. 1–6.

Chapter 10

1 'The day the world changed'. This cover headline in *The Economist* of 15 September 2001 typified the Western media reaction to 11 September.

2 Italian Prime Minister S. Berlusconi, 24 September 2001.

3 'Six months on. A balance-sheet', *The Economist*, 9 March 2002, pp. 11–12.

4 The target countries nominated by the Pentagon in the leaked classified document were the 'axis of evil' gang of three, plus China, Russia, Libya and Syria. The Nuclear Posture Review widened the circumstances thought to justify a possible nuclear response and expands the list of targets.

5 In contrast to the cool reception US Vice-President Cheney received from a number of Arab countries in his tour in March 2002, and criticism of a possible US attack on Iraq from some other EU leaders, the UK was markedly supportive. At a joint press conference with Vice-President Cheney on 11 March 2002 British Prime Minister Tony Blair stated: 'There is a threat from Saddam Hussein and the weapons of mass destruction that he has acquired. It is not in doubt at all.' A Downing Street source later said that 'no decisions' had been taken about military action against Iraq (*Independent*, 12 March 2002).

6 *Civiltà Cattolico*, January 2003. Official publication of the Vatican.

7 D. Frum, *The Right Man. The Surprise Presidency of George W. Bush*, New York: Random House, 2003, pp. 232–33.

8 See: STRATFOR, 24.6.02, *The Palestinian strategy,* 'The Palestinian strategy makes no sense except in the context of alignment with al-Qaeda . . . the goals of the Palestinians and those of al-Qaeda have converged.'

9 Camille Mansour, 'The impact of 11 September on the Israeli–Palestinian conflict', in *Journal of Palestinian Studies*, Vol. XXXI: 2, Winter 2002, p. 13.

10 Aluf Benn, *George Bush: Ariel Sharon's Most Powerful Weapon* http://www.salon.com/news/features/2002/03/08/weapon

11 SCR 1397, adopted on 12 March 2002, affirms 'a vision of a region where two states, Israel and Palestine, live side by side within secure and recognised borders'.

12 President G. W. Bush, White House Address, 14 March 2003.

13 *The Economist* of 23 March 2002 has an excellent survey of the social and economic problems faced by the Gulf monarchies.

Bibliography

Aburish, S. K. (2000) *Saddam Hussein. The Politics of Revenge*, London: Bloomsbury. His account of the Arab League summit of 30 and 31 May 1990 vividly illuminates the attitudes of the main players as the crisis deepened.

Alani, M. M. (1990) *Operation Vantage. British Military Intervention in Kuwait in 1961*, Surbiton: Laam Press. For anyone interested in the earlier Kuwait crisis.

BBC News *The Day that Shook the World*, London, BBC Worldwide Ltd, 2001. Correspondents reports on world-wide reaction to 11 September 2001. Written in the weeks following the al-Qaeda attacks.

Bresheeth, H. and Yuval-Davis, N. (eds) (1991) *The Gulf War and The New World Order*, London: Zed Books. Comprehensive collection of articles written at the time of the crisis with particular emphasis on anti-war issues and the global balance of power.

Chomsky, N. (2001) *9-11*, New York: Seven Stories Press. Series of short accounts of responses to the al-Qaeda attacks on America and US foreign policy in the Middle East.

Choueiri, Y. (1999) 'Essay on the history of the Lebanon', in *Middle East and North Africa 2000*, London: Europa. Authoritative and concise history.

Cordesman, A. (1996) *Perilous Prospects: The Peace Process and the Arab–Israeli Military Balance*, Boulder, Colo.: Westview Press. Useful text with expert analysis from a military and strategic perspective.

Ehteshami, A. and Nonneman, G. (eds) (1991) *War and Peace in the Gulf*, Reading, Mass.: Ithaca Press. This is one of the best studies for the specialist reader.

Eickelman, D. and Piscatori, J. (1996) *Muslim Politics*, Princeton: Princeton University Press. Excellent account of a diverse body of Muslim political voices from across the globe.

Esposito, J. L. (1992) *The Islamic Threat: Myth or Reality?*, Oxford: Oxford University Press. Strong account of the debate about modern Islamist movements and their impact on contemporary politics.

Esposito, J. L. (2002) *Unholy War: Terror in the Name of Islam*, New York: Oxford University Press. Authoritative explanation of the many dimensions of Muslim politics made manifest in the contemporary Middle East and beyond.

Fisk, R. (1990) *Pity the Nation*, London: Athenaeum. A vivid journalistic account of the civil war by a correspondent who has lived in the Lebanon for over twenty years. Good on atmosphere.

Fraser, T. (1995) *The Arab–Israeli Conflict*, Basingstoke: Macmillan. One of the best concise historical accounts available.

Freedman, L. and Karsh, E. (1993) *The Gulf Conflict 1990–1991*, London and Boston: Faber & Faber. The contrary argument to Rajaee's book. Saddam was reacting to Iranian provocation and had very limited war aims confined to deterring Khomeini and occupying small areas of Iran of strategic importance for Iraq's access to the Gulf.

Freedman, R. O. (1993) *The Middle East after Iraq's Invasion of Kuwait*, Gainesville, Fla.: University Press of Florida. This book has excellent essays on the policies pursued by the other main players, and the opening chapter, 'The Gulf War. A Political and Military Assessment', is a valuable analysis of the conflict.

Gerner, D. (1994) *One Land, Two Peoples: The Conflict over Palestine*, Boulder, Colo.: Westview Press. Lively and well-written text covering the many aspects of the Palestinian–Israeli conflict.

Halliday, F. (2001) *'Two Hours that Shook the World'. Sept 11 2001*, London: Saqi Press. Best 'instant book' on 9/11 and its likely consequences. Readable and perceptive.

Hourani, A. (1986) *Political Society in Lebanon: A Historical Introduction*, Cambridge, Mass.: Massachusetts Center for International Studies. Excellent scene-setter for the modern Lebanon.

el-Khazen, F. (2000) *The Breakdown of the State in Lebanon*, London: I.B. Tauris. For someone wanting to study the Lebanon in greater depth.

Kirisci, G. M. and Winrow, K. (eds) (1998) *The Kurdish Question and Turkey. An Example of a Trans-state in Ethnic Conflict*. London and Portland, Oreg.: Frank Cass. This is a very useful and balanced account of the Kurds within Turkey.

Kreyenbroek, P. G. and Sperl, S. (eds) (1992) *The Kurds. A Contemporary Overview*, London: Routledge. Excellent for further reading on the Kurdish issue.

Lesch, D. (ed.) (1996) *The Middle East and the United States*, Boulder, Colo.: Westview Press. Excellent analysis of US policy on the Gulf crisis and on earlier superpower confrontation.

Massoulié, F. (1999) *Middle East Conflicts*, New York: Interlink Publishing. Well-presented and profusely illustrated paperback with some coverage of the Lebanese civil war. A slightly 'tabloid' approach, but readable.

McDowell, D. (1997) *A Modern History of the Kurds*, London: I.B. Tauris. This is probably the best and most authoritative historical study of the Kurds in English and is easily accessible to the general reader.

Milton-Edwards, B. (1996) *Islamic Politics in Palestine*, London: I.B. Tauris. Overview of a century of Islamic activism in the Palestinian–Israeli arena.

Mojtahed-Zahed, P. (1999) *Security and Territoriality in the Persian Gulf*, Richmond, Surrey: Curzon. Despite some pro-Iranian partiality the book is very strong on Iraq–Iran tensions, including the Iraq–Iran confrontation of 1969–1975.

Pappe, I. (1994) *The Making of the Arab–Israeli Conflict 1947–1951*, London: I.B. Tauris. Strong and balanced account of the makings of conflict between Israel and its Arab neighbours, as well as the birth of the refugee issue for Palestinians.

Quandt, W. (1986) *Camp David, Peacemaking and Politics*, Washington: Brookings Institution. Strong analytical record of the forces employed to create peace between Israel and the Egyptians following the 1973 war.

Rabinovitch, I. (1991) *The Road Not Taken: Early Arab–Israeli Negotiations*, Oxford: Oxford University Press. Useful historical account and analysis of attempts at peacemaking in the region.

Rajaee, F. (ed.) (1993) *The Iran–Iraq War. The Politics of Aggression*, Gainesville, Fla.: University Press of Florida. The conflict from a strongly Iranian perspective. Lively essays.

Said, E. (1995) *The Politics of Dispossession: The Struggle for Palestinian Self-Determination*, London: Vintage. A very good and easily readable collection of articles and essays covering twenty years of Palestinian personalities and issues. Edward Said is a leading US-based Palestinian academic and one of the best living Arab writers on this topic.

Shehadi, N. and Hollis, R. (eds) (1996) *Lebanon on Hold: Implications for Middle East Peace*, London: RIIA. Good collection of articles with perspectives of post-war Lebanon and the challenge of reconstruction.

Smith, C. D. (1992) *Palestine and the Arab–Israeli Conflict*, Basingstoke: Macmillan. A good account of the roots of the conflict for a first-time reader.

Tessler, M. (1994) *A History of the Israeli–Palestinian Conflict*, Bloomington: Indiana University Press. Comprehensive and detailed account by foremost historian.

Tibi, B. (1998) *Conflict and War in the Middle East*, Basingstoke: Macmillan. Convincingly argued text on conflict in the region.

Usher, G. (1995) *Palestine in Crisis*, London: Pluto. Strong journalistic account of the post-Oslo era in the West Bank and Gaza Strip under the Palestinian National Authority.

Willis, M. (1996) *The Islamist Challenge in Algeria: A Political History*, Reading, Mass.: Ithaca Press. Strong account of the rise of Islamist forces in Algeria and the descent into civil violence in the 1990s.

Yapp, M. E. (1987) *The Making of the Modern Near East*, London: Longman. A concise summary of post-Second World War Lebanese history. Covers the historical background up to 1957.

Yapp, M. E. (1996) *The Near East Since the First World War*, London: Longman. Companion text to *The Making of the Modern Near East*, with sound historical focus.

Index

41, 52, 57, 78, 85; roots of
Islamophobia 50; war with Iraq 6,
40, 84–8, 97
Iraq: 'axis of evil' 120; Britain and
116; chemical attack on Kurds 91,
97–8; Cold War context 43, 45;
economic factors 112–13; finding
links to al-Qaeda 120–1; Gulf War
36, 37; Hashemite overthrow 66;
invades Kuwait 32–3, 95, 97–9,
99–103; Kurds and 72, 78–80, 83;
military power 89–90, 98;
Operation Desert Storm 100–5; and
the PLO 98; Shi'ite population 103;
UN sanctions against 46; US
campaign against 6, 121–4; use of
'human shields' 102; war with Iran
6, 40, 84–8, 97; weapons of mass
destruction 120, 122–3 *see also*
Saddam Hussein
Islam: concept of jihad 58; groups in
Lebanon 62; and Iranian revolution
50; Iraq-Iran differences 88, 89, 90;
Kurds and 74; peacemakers of
50–1; political Islamism 52–9;
reductive view of 5, 49–51, 57–9,
106; resurgence of 52–3; Shi'a
characteristics 57; Sunnis and Shi'as
77, 78–9
Islamic Jihad 31–2, 54–5, 68
Islamic Salvation Army 56
Islamism: Al-Qaeda attacks on USA
118–19; in Algeria 55–6, 59; in
Egypt 53–4; Palestinian groups
54–5; variety of contexts 52–3
Israel: 1967 war 15–16; birth of 12–13,
25–7; conflict mentality 109;
economy of 112, 128; effect of
Kuwait invasion 32–3; expansion
27–8; international opinion 31, 32;
Iraqi missile attacks 102, 103; and
Lebanon 67–9; Madrid talks 33;
Oslo Accords 34; outbreak of
Intifada 30–2; peace movements
within 32; relations with US 38–9;
rise of state 10–13; 'road map'
challenge 34–5; roots of Palestinian
conflict 22–7; treatment of Arabs
within 25, 26, 29–31; treaty with
Egypt 8, 106; worries about Iraq 98

Israeli Defence Force (IDF) 10, 12

Jamaat al-Jihad 53
Jerusalem 26, 27
The Jewish State (Herzl) 23
Jewish Zionist Diaspora 28
Jews: anti-Semitism and 24; Holocaust
and 12, 25; Zionist movement
10–11, 23–6 *see also* Israel
Jordan: 1967 war 15; Cold War context
46; economics and peace 112; Iraq
and 90; and Jerusalem 26; and
Kuwait invasion 101, 102, 103–4;
Palestinians and 13, 28–9, 104
Jumblatt family 63

Karsh, E. 26
Khalidi, R. 31
Khomeini, Ayatollah Ruhollah 41, 52,
57, 78, 93–4
Khrushchev, Nikita 42
Kissinger, Henry 106
Kurdish Democratic Party (KDP) 79
Kurdish Democratic Party of Iran
(KDPI) 76–7
Kurds 2, 5–6; chemical attack on 91,
97–8; Iran and 76–8; Iraq and
78–80, 83, 87, 91; Iraq-Iran conflict
90; and Kurdistan 74, 77;
population and distribution 72–4;
religion of 74, 78; Republic of
Mahabad 77; 'safe haven' for 80,
103; Turkey and 74–6, 80–3
Kuwait 85, 87; autocratic monarchy
101, 104; economic factors 113;
expels Palestinians 104; Iraq
invades 2, 6, 32–3, 45, 95, 97–9,
99–103; Iraq-Iran conflict 90; Iraqi
debts to 90; Operation Desert Storm
100, 102–5

Lausanne, Treaty of 75–6
League of Nations 11
Lebanon 2, 5; Charter of National
Conciliation 69; civil war 67–9; and
Cold War strategies 40; divided
society of 60–5; economy of 112;
fedayeen attacks on Israel 18;
Hizballah 57; independence 64;
Islamic resistance movements 10;